INTEGRITY
MANAGEMENT

INTEGRITY MANAGEMENT

A Guide to Managing
Legal and Ethical
Issues in the Workplace

Debbie Thorne LeClair
O. C. Ferrell
John P. Fraedrich

University of Tampa Press
Tampa, Florida
1998

Manufactured in the United States of America
First Edition

The University of Tampa Press
401 West Kennedy Boulevard
Tampa, Florida 33606

ISBN: 1-879852-55-1

Library of Congress Cataloging-in-Publication Data

LeClair, Debbie Thorne, 1966-
    Integrity management : a guide to managing legal and ethical
    issues in the workplace / Debbie Thorne LeClair, O.C. Ferrell, John P.
    Fraedrich. — 1st ed.
        p. cm.
    Includes bibliographical references and index.
    ISBN 1-879852-55-1
    1. Business ethics. 2. Integrity. 3. Management—Moral and
ethical aspects. I. Ferrell, O.C. II. Fraedrich, John P.
III. Title.
HF5387.L434 1998
658—dc21   97-21063
                                                    CIP

This Book Is Dedicated To:

My parents Jim and Mary Helen Thorne and my husband Daniel
Debbie Thorne LeClair

My wife Linda and my son James
O. C. Ferrell

My wife Debbie and my children, Anna,
Jacob, Joshua, and Lael
John P. Fraedrich

CONTENTS

ACKNOWLEDGMENTS

We wish to acknowledge the many talented individuals who helped make this book a reality. We offer special thanks to our editor, Gwyneth M. Vaughn, who played a major role in organizing and refining chapter content. Barbara Gilmer assisted with editing and provided helpful advice and support. Jack K. Gray shared many insights related to the implications of the Federal Sentencing Guidelines for Organizations and the importance of compliance programs. Tess Kristensen and Marnie McGlathery played a major role in the design and development of our World Wide Web site. Many thanks to Wendy Plant, Rita Burkhardt, Claudia Haggerty and Marisol Paradoa for their technical assistance, research, and general support for this book project.

University President Ronald L. Vaughn created the Center for Ethics in 1989 and provides ongoing support. The University of Tampa College of Business Dean Alfred N. Page continues to provide guidance to the Center for Ethics. Stephen Stumpf, Dean of Professional Development at Booz·Allen & Hamilton Inc., encouraged us to write this book. Linda Ferrell, Assistant Professor of Management, was involved in every aspect of the book and is responsible for contributing both content and support. Many thanks also to Richard Mathews, Director of The University of Tampa Press, and to Ana Montalvo and Ellen White for their help with this book's publication.

Debbie Thorne LeClair and O. C. Ferrell appreciate the encouragement and support from colleagues at the University of Tampa, the guidance of the Center for Ethics Advisory Board, and many companies' willingness to share their experiences with us. John Fraedrich acknowledges the help and support of colleagues at Southern Illinois University.

PREFACE

Every day, it seems, *The Wall Street Journal*, *USA Today*, and your local newspaper report the scandalous activities of organizations. Many of these scandals stem from misconduct resulting from a failure to incorporate integrity into organizational policies. Without programs to manage organizational integrity effectively, ethical concerns often turn into legal problems for organizations, which destroy trust with the public, customers, and other stakeholders.

Integrity Management is a trade book designed for managers who are concerned about legal and ethical responsibilities in the workplace. Anyone with managerial responsibility needs to understand and respond to integrity issues. The quality of relationships with employees and customers depends on an ethical climate and clear understanding of legal risks. While many people feel that being ethical and obeying the law are just common sense, the complexity of relationships in our society requires that we protect ourselves from losing the trust of others and the possibility of costly civil and criminal litigation.

We have therefore developed this book as a guide to managing integrity in the workplace. We believe that creating an ethical organizational culture which understands and responds to integrity challenges will prevent misconduct and negative headlines. However, the development of a high-integrity corporate culture does not happen overnight, and it requires that organizations move beyond a legalistic approach to decision making. Only through an uncompromising commitment to the implementation of both legal *and* ethical principles can integrity become a meaningful force in organizational success.

While our approach is practical, the concepts in this book are based on the latest research and best practices available to develop effective programs for managing integrity. We bring to this endeavor more than 50 years of combined experience in the field of organizational ethics and compliance. We have managed businesses, served as consultants and expert witnesses, educated thousands of business students, and conducted research on organizational integrity. We have assembled our knowledge and experience into a format that can guide you through integrity strategy development and program implementation.

In this book we offer insights into definitions, issues, and frameworks useful for understanding the various factors that influence ethical and legal decision making in the organization. We explore legal pressures for ethical compliance, particularly the Federal Sentencing Guidelines for Organizations, which have a profound impact on organizational conduct. We also examine the steps involved in developing an effective organizational integrity program, including specific direction on implementing ethics and legal compliance training. Because of the increasingly international nature of business and communications, we also explore the complexities of integrity management in a global economy. Later, we'll take a more external perspective and consider what it takes to become a "good citizen organization" by linking internal ethics compliance initiatives to the integrity concerns of society and other relevant constituencies. We also take a look at the initiatives and "best practices" of five organizations that we believe have demonstrated great commitment, creativity, and effectiveness in their efforts to develop integrity programs. Finally, we include in each chapter a brief checklist to help you analyze the strengths and weaknesses of your organization's progress in managing ethical and legal issues.

We believe this guide represents a major breakthrough in the world of trade books. To help you stay up to date and to provide additional insights on integrity management, we maintain a World Wide Web site that includes cases, useful examples, and implementation linkages for each of our ten chapters. (Point your browser at http://www.utampa.edu/acad/cob/cfe/orginteg.htm). This Web site provides a continuous flow of new ideas to help you improve your organization's integrity efforts. We recommend that you use the Web site to find additional information on chapters that are of particular importance to you in assessment or program development. This Web site makes the book interactive, so please feel free to E-Mail us and communicate about effective integrity initiatives in your organization. If you need additional information or would like to develop customized compliance materials for your organization, we will be glad to assist you.

Debbie Thorne LeClair
O. C. Ferrell
John P. Fraedrich   August 1997

CHAPTER ONE

MANAGING INTEGRITY

Integrity is one of the most important, yet perhaps most misunderstood, concerns in the world of work today.
— Debbie Thorne LeClair

The two cornerstones of integrity are legal compliance and ethical conduct.
— O.C. Ferrell

Integrity is based on the character and core values of an organization.
— John Fraedrich

▼ A large industrial agricultural products manufacturer pays $100 million in organizational fines after a lengthy, highly publicized federal investigation into a price-fixing scheme.

▼ A book wholesaler allegedly programs its computers to systematically overcharge government libraries, automatically rescinding promised discounts when customers' purchases are entered into the database. When customers complain, sales personnel are instructed to describe the charges as mistakes and adjust the computers so that particular client is not overbilled again.

▼ After analyzing several race-discrimination lawsuits, an Internet legal advice service recommends that companies routinely destroy documents, sign confidentiality agreements with subordinates, and prohibit workers from taping conversations.

▼ A coworker advising a new employee on how to fill out
expense forms offers this advice on how to get reimbursed for
expense items not listed on the forms: "You can't include tips,
so one way you can be reimbursed is by increasing the amount
on your cab fares. As you see, most cab drivers stamp the re-
ceipt and let you fill in the amount. I have been with the company for five years, and I should know what's okay to do."

These incidents represent real world integrity issues. You can probably think of more examples based on your own observations and experiences in the workplace. Headlines in your local newspaper, *USA
Today, The Wall Street Journal, Fortune,* and *Business Week* spotlight
the growing importance of integrity in the workplace. Many of these
headlines stem from misconduct resulting from a failure to incorporate integrity into organizational policies.

To us, *integrity management* is an organization's uncompromising implementation of legal and ethical principles. An organization
should include integrity in its strategic planning to provide a complete focus on productivity and success. We therefore decided to
develop this book as a guide to planning, organizing, and implementing organizational integrity. We want to help managers in all
types of organizations comply with laws and regulations by offering a blueprint for improving integrity in the workplace. We believe that integrity management ultimately improves organizational
character and increases most measures of trust, customer service,
productivity, and profits.

Before we proceed, we think it is important to tell you what this book
does and does not do. First, this book is a guide for organizational
integrity, not personal ethics. Second, it does not moralize or tell you
what is right or wrong in specific situations. Third, although the book
discusses integrity and decision-making processes, we do not advocate
any particular philosophy or process as the best or most ethical. Rather,
our goal is to help you understand and apply your current values and
convictions to decisions and to encourage you to think about the consequences of your decisions on business and society. We want to help you
develop integrity programs and resolve ethical and legal issues. The framework we develop in this book therefore focuses on processes for integrity

management—implementing a legal and ethical compliance program.

Anyone who says that creating a high-integrity workplace is easy does not understand the challenges and pressures that most of us face as we make decisions on a daily basis. This book is about creating an organizational culture of integrity to help deal with those challenges and achieve professional and organizational success. To get started on the road toward organizational integrity, we will explore in this chapter the growing importance and rewards of managing integrity in today's organizations.

WHY IS MANAGING ORGANIZATIONAL INTEGRITY IMPORTANT?

Integrity is one of the most important, yet perhaps most misunderstood, concerns in the workplace today. There is conclusive evidence that the failure to manage integrity costs companies billions of dollars in fines, litigation, increased costs, and, perhaps most important of all, lost customer relationships. Companies are suing competitors over allegations of unfair pricing, deceptive advertising, trademark and copyright infringement, and monopolistic practices in order to level the field of business. Consumers are demanding greater social and environmental awareness from the organizations they patronize, support, and in which they invest. Federal, state, and local governments are responding to misconduct with increasing regulations, standards, and business accountability. The costs of unethical and fraudulent acts committed by working Americans on a daily basis currently total $400 billion annually. Examples of these acts include making unauthorized photocopies and long-distance calls, taking office supplies home, using company stamps to send personal mail, taking bogus sick days, and misappropriating cash and inventory.[1] Yet, economic downturns, downsizings, and pressure to increase profits often put integrity on the back burner at work.

By its very nature, organizational integrity is controversial, and there is no universally accepted approach for resolving questions. However, many groups in society, including government, are encouraging organizational accountability for ethical and legal conduct. Organizations are being asked to prevent and control misconduct by implementing ethics and legal compliance programs. Integrity brings many rewards to organizations that nurture it, but managing integrity requires activity and attention on several levels—complying with the law, setting ethical standards, and being a good organizational citizen in society.

Organizational Ethics

Ethics has been called the study and philosophy of human conduct, with an emphasis on the determination of right and wrong. For managers, ethics at work refers to rules or standards governing the conduct of organizational members. Most definitions of ethics relate to rules, standards, and principles as to what is right or wrong in specific situations. For our purposes and in simple terms, *organizational ethics* refers to generally accepted standards that guide behavior in business and other organizational contexts.

One difference between an ordinary decision and an ethical one is that accepted rules may not apply and the decision maker must weigh values in a situation that he or she may not have faced before. Another difference is the amount of emphasis placed on a person's values when making an ethical decision. Whether a specific behavior is right or wrong, ethical or unethical, is often determined by the mass media, interest groups, the legal system, and individuals' personal morals. While these groups are not necessarily "right," their judgments influence society's acceptance or rejection of an organization and its activities. Consequently, values, judgments, and complex situations all play a critical role in ethical decision making.

Most people would agree that high ethical standards require both organizations and individuals to conform to sound moral principles. However, a couple of special factors must be considered when applying ethics to business organizations. First, to survive, businesses must obviously make a profit. Second, businesses must balance their desire for profits against the needs and desires of society. Maintaining this balance often requires compromises or tradeoffs. To address these unique aspects, society has developed rules—both legal and implicit— to guide owners, managers, and employees in their efforts to earn profits in ways that do not harm individuals or society as a whole.

Organizational practices and policies often create pressures, opportunities, and incentives that may sway employees to make unethical decisions. We've all seen news articles describing some "decent, hard-working family person" who engaged in illegal or unethical activities. Sometimes, these articles allude to an unethical corporate culture that either encouraged or ignored the unethical behavior. A study by the Ethics Resource Center found that 29 percent of employees surveyed felt pressured by management to compromise their standards of ethical conduct to meet business objectives.[2] In other words, the integrity standards we learn at home, school, and in the community do not always prepare us for the intricacies of the business world and the pressures of work.

The Good Citizen Organization and Social Responsibility

At the first symposium on corporate crime in America sponsored by the United States Sentencing Commission, Chairman Richard Conaboy encouraged businesses to create the "good citizen corporation." The commission's message was clear—if corporations commit to high standards of integrity and carefully develop and implement policies that deter misconduct, then the government will not have to be as involved in regulation and enforcement. The commission's mechanism for encouraging such citizenship was to codify into law incentives for organizations to take crime-deterring actions through the establishment of rigorous, effective internal compliance programs.

We believe that taking a purely legalistic approach to creating the good citizen organization will fail. Before they can achieve integrity, organizations must understand their culture, including employee ideas, daily patterns of behavior, and values that are used to cope with problems. Putting it another way, organizational culture is the glue that holds an organization together and expresses the values, ethical climate, social ideals, and the approaches members use to make ethical and legal decisions. So, an attempt to manage organizational culture by focusing on just legal compliance is incomplete. The *socially responsible* organization recognizes an obligation to maximize positive effects and minimize negative effects on society. The "good citizen corporation" should be unimpaired in contributing to society by exercising economic, legal, ethical, and, we hope, philanthropic responsibilities.

Rewards and Challenges

So far, we've tended to focus more on the downside of unethical organizational activities. On a more positive note, ethical and socially responsible behavior can have many rewards. First, when employees perceive their organization as having high integrity, they are more likely to be committed and satisfied in their work. An ethical organizational culture fosters employees' trust which is passed on to customers, suppliers, and other clients. Second, organizations that are perceived as ethical and socially responsible often have a strong and loyal customer base. A national survey indicated that three out of four consumers are avoiding or refusing to buy from certain businesses because of misconduct.[3] A survey by Cone Communications and Roper Starch Worldwide found that 54 percent of respondents would pay more for a product that supports a cause they care about; 66 percent said they would switch brands, and 62 percent said they would switch retailers, to support a cause they care about. Yet another study found that nearly 90 percent of consumers surveyed would be more likely to buy from the company that has the best reputation for social responsibility when quality, service, and price are otherwise equal among competitors.[4]

These attitudes contribute to our third point, that there is growing evidence that ethical companies are also profitable ones. We do know that some companies' profits have declined after misconduct is publicized. Bausch & Lomb, for example, watched its earnings fall 54 percent after managers "played fast and loose with accounting principles and ethics."[5] Finally, many organizations that have experienced long-term success acknowledge the role ethics has played in their longevity. The reasons listed above provide a convincing rationale for the positive relationship between ethics and organizational success.

The essential place to begin evaluating the rewards of workplace integrity is to determine employee attitudes toward legal compliance and ethical conduct. Dr. Terry Loe, a professor at Baylor University, has found that employees' perception of legal and ethical compliance is associated with increased levels of trust, commitment to quality, and a market orientation.[6] Firms that have greater levels of trust function more efficiently and are more productive on a daily basis. Employees committed to customer service and the quality of products should provide a competitive advantage. Furthermore, a high level of market orientation and associated high integrity can potentially increase organizational performance by improving employees' responsiveness to the market and customer needs. This responsiveness often includes a focus on organizational relationships that require expectations for behavior that are higher than industry or government standards. These actions that "go beyond the law" usually fall into the category of ethical decisions, or those based on core values that promote a good citizen organization. Important measures of success, including profits, should be the result of integrity efforts to enhance legal and ethical compliance.

Understanding workplace integrity is valuable for many other reasons. Many people believe that if an organization hires good, ethical people, then it will be a good "corporate citizen." However, an individual's personal values and moral philosophies are but one factor in the decision-making process about potential legal and ethical problems. True, moral rules can be related to a variety of situations in life, and some people do not distinguish everyday ethical issues from those that occur on the job. Our concern, however, is with the application of rules and principles in a work environment.

Just being a good person and, in your own view, having sound personal ethics may not be sufficient to handle the integrity issues that arise in the workplace. It is important to recognize the relationship between legal and ethical decisions. While abstract virtues such as honesty, fairness, and openness are often assumed to be self-evident and accepted by all employees, a high level of personal moral development may not prevent an individual from violating the law in an organizational context, where even experienced lawyers debate the exact meaning of the law. Some organizational ethics perspectives assume that ethics training is for people who have unacceptable personal moral development, but that is not necessarily the case. Because organizations are comprised of diverse individuals whose personal values should be respected, a collective agreement on workplace integrity is as vital as other managerial decisions. For example, would your organization expect to achieve its strategic mission without communicating this goal to employees? Would your firm expect to implement a quality management system without educating every employee on his or her role in the process? In our view, integrity needs to be treated similarly—with clear expectations as to what comprises legal and ethical conduct.

Many people who have limited work experience suddenly find themselves making decisions about product quality, advertising, pricing, hiring practices, and pollution control. The values they learned from family, religion, and school may not provide specific guidelines for these complex decisions, especially when the realities of work objectives, group decision making, and other issues come into play. Many ethics decisions are close calls. Years of experience in a particular industry may be required to know what is acceptable.

Even if you are experienced, knowing more about workplace integrity will help you identify both legal and ethical issues and recognize and manage the decision processes for resolving them. By focusing on this area, you will be in a better position to assist employees and your organization with conflicts between personal values and the objectives and needs that guide work behavior. Finally, this book will expose you to the types of programs, policies, training, and creative approaches that promote integrity in organizations.

THE EVOLUTION OF WORKPLACE INTEGRITY

Although this book focuses on the role of integrity in many types of organizations, it is helpful to examine the changing nature of ethics in business organizations as it has evolved over the twentieth century.

Before 1960, there were many questions raised about wages, labor practices, and consumer health and welfare, as well as the morality of capitalism. Many of these issues were debated from the perspectives of humanistic values versus materialistic goals of organizations. While legislation was passed to protect the health of consumers and improve working conditions for employees, integrity was discussed more from a political, theological, and personal perspective.

During the 1960s, society turned to causes. An antibusiness attitude developed as many critics attacked the vested interests that controlled the economic and political sides of society. The 1960s saw the decay of the inner cities and the growth of ecological problems. The mood of this period was captured in President John F. Kennedy's four basic human rights—the right to safety, the right to be informed, the right to choose, and the right to be heard—which came to be known as the Consumer's Bill of Rights. The consumer movement is generally believed to have begun in 1965 with the publication of Ralph Nader's *Unsafe at Any Speed,* which characterized the auto industry as putting profit and style ahead of lives and safety.

The 1970s saw integrity directly applied to many business activities. Colleges of business and philosophers entered the arena, applying ethical theory and philosophical analysis to business ethics. Companies became more concerned with their public image, and as social demands grew, many businesses realized that they had to address ethical issues more directly. The government got more involved through regulatory activities, and legislation to control business activities increased dramatically. For example, the Federal Trade Commission Act of 1975 gave the FTC more power to prohibit unfair industry practices. Issues such as deceptive advertising, product safety, and antitrust became more prominent in government enforcement activities. In addition, a number of environmental protection laws were enacted, including the Clean Air Act (1970), National Environmental Policy Act (1970), Coastal Zone Management Act (1972), Federal Water Pollution Control Act (1972), Noise Pollution Control Act (1972), and the Toxic Substances Control Act (1976).

In the 1980s businesses took action to improve and support organizational integrity efforts. Colleges across the country offered hundreds of courses in business ethics, with more than 40,000 students enrolled. Centers of business ethics offered publications, courses, conferences, and seminars. Integrity was also a prominent concern among leading companies, such as General Electric Co., The Chase Manhattan Corporation, General Motors, Atlantic Richfield Co., Caterpillar Inc., and S. C. Johnson & Son, Inc. Many of these firms established ethics committees and social policy committees to address ethics and integrity issues.

The 1980s also ushered in the Reagan/Bush political eras, with the accompanying belief that self-regulation, rather than regulation by government, was in the public's best interest. With the easing and removal of many trade barriers, companies merged and divested within an increasingly global atmosphere. Many corporations expanded globally and found themselves mired in foreign value structures where accepted rules of business behavior no longer applied. Thus, while business schools were offering courses in business ethics, the rules of business were changing at a phenomenal rate because of less regulation. While companies had more freedom to make decisions, the government was developing new mandatory guidelines to control firms that were involved in misconduct.

In 1986 eighteen defense contractors drafted the Defense Industry Initiative on Business Ethics and Conduct (DII) to guide corporate support for ethical conduct.[7] By 1996, 55 members, representing more than 50 percent of the prime contractors with the U.S. Department of Defense, had signed on. DII established principles to promote ethical conduct and a forum for members to discuss the best tactics to link business practices and policies to successful ethical compliance. This initiative would later become the foundation for the Federal Sentencing Guidelines for Organizations, which we'll look at next.[8]

The federal government created the United States Sentencing Commission to institutionalize ethical compliance programs and help prevent illegal activity. Its *Federal Sentencing Guidelines for Organizations (FSGO),* approved by Congress in 1991, broke new ground by codifying into law incentives for organizations to develop effective internal compliance programs to prevent misconduct.[9] Of critical importance is the fact that these guidelines hold businesses accountable for the crimes of their employees. The sentencing guidelines take a carrot-and-stick approach. Companies that lack effective ethical compliance programs can incur severe penalties if their employees violate the law. And we do mean severe: Several firms, including Daiwa Bank of Japan and Archer Daniels Midland, have been disciplined with fines exceeding $100 million for the illegal activities of their employees. However, by taking action to establish high ethical standards and thereby prevent misconduct in the first place, a company can get the carrot by possibly avoiding harsh penalties should one of its employees break the law.[10] Taking a mechanical approach using legalistic logic is not sufficient to avert serious penalties. A company must develop corporate values, enforce its own code of ethics, strive to prevent misconduct, and, in short, be a "good citizen" corporation.[11]

While the 1980s were watershed years for the public's awareness and dismay at unscrupulous business practices, the 1990s have become a decade of ethics training, ethical compliance programs, and ethics consulting, which is now a $1 billion industry.[12] Heightened public sensitivity to business ethics, along with the Federal Sentencing Guidelines, has convinced many companies to incorporate ethics into strategic planning and day-to-day operations. By the mid 1990s, more than 80 percent of large companies had codes of conduct, and over one-third of major U.S. companies had an ethics officer,[13] and these numbers are increasing daily. NYNEX Corp., for example, created an ethics department that has trained 95,000 past and present employees, sent managers to full-day workshops, and presented "tailgate packages" to employees in trucks, offices, and lunchrooms. NYNEX tailors these presentations to address ethical situations specific to each group.[14]

Thus, through laws and policies, the government has placed the responsibility for integrity squarely on the shoulders of organizations and their managers. This responsibility usually entails developing a compliance program and code of ethics or conduct, conducting employee training, and creating an organizational culture that is conducive to ethical decision making. Businesses, nonprofit entities, and other organizations must be aware of the expected ethical standards or their ability to achieve their objectives may be diminished. In an age of increasing accountability, organizations must demonstrate integrity to many groups including consumers, government, stockholders, and other publics. Otherwise, they may face scrutiny in the media, lawsuits, consumer complaints, decreasing market share, and general distrust and dissatisfaction. These issues can cause financial difficulties and long-term image problems for organizations.

YOUR GUIDE TO INTEGRITY MANAGEMENT

Integrity, including both ethical and legal issues, will continue to be at the forefront of organizational concerns as managers and employees face increasingly complex decisions in the twenty-first century. An organizational integrity effort establishes formal accountability and responsibility for appropriate organizational conduct. An effective program has the potential to encourage all employees to understand organizational values and ethical climate and to comply with policies and codes of conduct that create a good citizen organization. It takes into account values, ethics, and legal requirements, helping an organization develop trust and prevent misconduct.

While many books focus on moral philosophy and the improvement of personal ethics, our approach is to help you implement integrity as a manager or as an employee within an organization. We view that many integrity issues are complex and have both a legal and an ethical dimension. Therefore, we have tried to avoid separating legal and ethical issues. Certainly issues such as sexual harassment, bribery, fraud, and price fixing have their legal dimensions, but there are many gray areas and legal issues which often result from ethical deficiencies in making daily decisions about doing the right thing. Essentially, we believe that by *focusing on ethical behavior,* your organization can improve its chances of *avoiding legal problems.* Although legal issues may arise that are beyond management's control, an organizational focus on ethics and integrity can substantially reduce its vulnerability to such liability.

In this book, we have provided a guide for improving legal and ethical workplace practices. In Chapter 2 we focus on identifying ethical and legal issues in the workplace, and in Chapter 3 we provide a framework for understanding the various factors that influence organizational decisions to resolve these issues. Because organizational culture is so important in the development of workplace integrity, we devote Chapter 4 to this topic. Chapter 5 is a basic primer on the Federal Sentencing Guidelines for Organizations and their effect on organizational practices. In Chapter 6, we provide suggestions for creating an effective legal compliance and ethics program based on the seven recommended steps from the sentencing guidelines. Chapter 7 extends Chapter 6 by describing training techniques and tools that may be used to communicate and reinforce compliance and ethics expectations. Because integrity is a global issue, Chapter 8 examines the complexities of operating across national boundaries and within different countries. Chapter 9 takes a somewhat more external focus by exploring obligations to society and what it takes to create a good citizen organization. Chapter 10 highlights the ethics, social responsibility, and compliance initiatives of five organizations that have demonstrated commitment, effectiveness, success, and creativity in their efforts to implement workplace integrity. Finally, at the end of each chapter, you will find an Integrity Manager Checklist to help determine your organization's progress in various components of workplace integrity.

We believe that this guide to legal and ethical workplace practices provides comprehensive directions for anyone who has responsibilities in implementing or managing compliance efforts. Throughout this book, you will see how the increasing complexity of the law, work environment, and societal expectations require that organizations continuously define, communicate, monitor, and enforce standards of behavior. Because of these new complexities, we believe that all employees need to re-examine their understanding of how legal, ethical, and socially responsible decisions occur. Further, just as quality management principles have become commonplace, we believe that all organizations will soon have formal approaches to managing integrity. Perhaps we could call it Total Integrity Management (TIM).

All managers have the responsibility of due diligence in carrying out their companies' policies ethically, while complying with laws and regulations. As responsible members of society, we can never abdicate our personal, ethical, and social obligations to uphold basic moral ideals. Therefore, anyone who manages other employees needs to understand the concepts and frameworks for improving integrity. To assist your continuing efforts, we are maintaining a Web site at the Center for Ethics at The University of Tampa to support your interest and development in integrity management. On this site, you will find links to other organizations and information sources that will help keep you up-to-date on integrity management issues.

INTEGRITY MANAGER CHECKLIST

The following questions will give you a better understanding of where your organization stands with regard to workplace integrity. A large number of no responses indicates the need to re-examine your firm's approach to legal, ethical, and societal expectations.

YES NO

❏   ❏   Has your organization integrated legal concerns into the strategic planning process?

❏   ❏   Has your organization integrated its core ethical values into the strategic planning process?

❏   ❏   Has your organization integrated philanthropic activities into the strategic planning process?

❏   ❏   Does your organization have a commitment to contributing to the economic well-being of your community?

❏   ❏   Does your organization understand that integrity management requires internal planning and control?

❏   ❏   Do you have an organizational culture where managers take responsibility for encouraging integrity at work?

❏   ❏   Have employees in your organization developed a consensus as to what constitutes integrity at work?

❏   ❏   Do top managers in your organization openly communicate that integrity will positively affect financial performance?

❏   ❏   Do top managers encourage employees to balance the need to reach organizational objectives with the goal of being a good citizen organization?

❏   ❏   Does your organization have an integrity/compliance program based on the criteria established by the Federal Sentencing Guidelines for Organizations?

CHAPTER TWO

IDENTIFYING ETHICAL AND LEGAL ISSUES IN THE WORKPLACE

"In our working lives, we often experience situations where the 'right thing to do' is not immediately apparent. Loyalties—to our fellow employees, to managers, customers and suppliers, to our families, our communities, the environment, the corporation as a whole, and to ourselves—may seem to conflict. When we're faced with a complicated situation, it can be difficult to decide where the ethical path lies."

– Northern Telecom (Nortel), *Acting with Integrity,* found at www.nortel.com

Brian Choi owns a small grocery store in Atlanta's racially tense West End. In an area where Korean merchants have been cursed and worse for overcharging customers and not contributing to the community, Choi's Handy Supermarket is known for keeping its meat market open until midnight and its relatively competitive prices. Most of Choi's African-American customers are struggling to make ends meet, and many expect their young children to work to help out their families. So when Willie and Maurice Mathews, then aged 11 and 12, began hanging around the store and begging for work, Choi allowed the boys to carry bags for customers and run errands, after first securing their parents' permission. Choi was impressed with the boys' persistence, and he hoped his store would become a "sanctuary" of sorts for the boys, keeping them off the tough streets of the West End. For his efforts to make a difference in the boys' lives, Choi was recently fined $2,875 for violating U.S. child labor laws and ordered to pay $5,386 in back wages. He now turns away Willie and Maurice when they come by after school. "I've really never changed my mind about helping other youngsters, but I don't know any other way," he says.

Most executives, managers, and employees strive for organizational integrity and will never be associated with a scandal or punished for breaking the law. However, even ethical people encounter complex problems and issues that may be tough to resolve during the course of their careers. While Mr. Choi, as a businessman, should have known that employing children under age 14 is illegal in the United States, who among us cannot at least sympathize with his decision to give in to two children begging for odd jobs in a tough neighborhood where youngsters routinely work to help their families make ends meet?

One of the first steps toward understanding integrity in organizations is learning to recognize ethical and legal issues. We define an *ethical issue* as a problem, situation, or opportunity that requires an individual or organization to choose among several actions that may be judged by others as right or wrong, ethical or unethical. *Legal issues* are usually the result of ethical issues that have gone unchecked or without action on the part of employers, management, or even customers. Legal issues often stem from a lack of knowledge. When employees begin to work in a new industry, they often have little experience with the specific laws and regulations that govern their new work activities. Obviously, it is nearly impossible for all employees to understand the volumes of federal, state, local, and international law that may affect your organization. Brian Choi apparently didn't. However, every organization—from the smallest grocery to the largest multinational corporation—needs a system for monitoring the laws, regulations, and possible legislation that affect decision making in the workplace.

In the following chapters we provide a framework for organizing a system that focuses on both ethical and legal issues. But first, we take a look at how, why, and when these issues arise. Once ethical and legal issues of any sort have been identified, individuals and organizations must decide how to resolve them. Familiarity with the ethical issues that frequently arise in organizations may help you identify and resolve them when they occur. This understanding will assist you in developing codes of conduct, ethical compliance programs, and a focus on organizational integrity.

CONFLICT

Ethical and legal issues typically arise because of conflicts among individuals' personal moral philosophies and values, the values and attitudes of the firms in which they work, and those of the society in which they live. For instance, questions of integrity may stem from conflicts between consumers' demands for safe, quality products and manufacturers' desire to earn adequate profits. A manager's desire to hire specific employees whom he or she likes may conflict with the organization's belief in hiring the most qualified candidates and with society's aim to offer equal opportunity to women and minorities. How such conflicts are resolved may create ethical or legal issues for your organization.

People often experience conflict between their own moral values and their obligations to the organizations in which they work. Research suggests that many people perceive a difference between the ethical standards they use at home and those they apply at work.[2] This tension may be exacerbated when employees feel that their company pressures them to engage in unethical conduct. One survey of *Fortune* 500 firms found that 29 percent of respondents said they felt pressured by management to compromise standards of ethical conduct to meet business objectives.[3] Conflict may occur on several levels—between organizational goals and values and individuals' goals and values, between the organization's ethical values and integrity policy and organizational objectives, or between societal expectations and the company's need to reach its goals.

To resolve such conflicts in the workplace, employees need specific guidance on responding to situations that threaten organizational integrity. Identifying and classifying ethical and legal issues provides a good starting point for this guidance. Even the most seasoned readers will find this simple guide to classifying issues useful for "rethinking" how to organize and improve a concerted integrity and ethical compliance initiative. We have also provided a number of examples to demonstrate how even "good" organizations may experience ethical and legal problems.

CLASSIFICATION OF ETHICAL AND LEGAL ISSUES

Surveys of executives and employees by think tanks and the media provide an overview of unsettled issues in many industries. However, we think classifying issues as they relate to most organizations will help you better understand and create mechanisms to resolve them. We first examine issues in the context of three categories: honesty and fairness, communications, and conflicts of interest. In the next section we'll take a closer look at how these issues relate to the various functions and participants of organizational life. These categories obviously are *not* all inclusive, but they do offer a starting point for your organization's identification and control of relevant issues. These categories in no way reflect every issue that you might face; however, an effective assessment of your organization's and industry's major issues can be patterned after these categories.

Honesty and Fairness

At a minimum, employees, managers, and other organizational agents are expected to obey all applicable laws and regulations. In addition, they should not knowingly harm customers, clients, employees, or competitors through deception, misrepresentation, or coercion. Although people often act in their own economic self-interest, workplace relationships should be grounded on fairness, justice, and trust. Buyers should be able to trust sellers, and lenders should be able to trust borrowers. Failure to live up to these expectations destroys trust and makes it difficult, if not impossible, to continue relationships and exchanges.[4]

Lying raises ethical issues because it destroys trust. Some business students may be learning in an environment where a "little exaggeration" is used to improve the prestige and academic ranking of their university. For example, *The Wall Street Journal* exposed some universities' practices of inflating Scholastic Aptitude Test (SAT) scores and graduation rates when supplying information for popular guidebooks, such as *Money*'s *College Guide*. In some cases, admission departments were found to have lied to rating agencies, fabricated SAT data, and deliberately misled alumni and incoming students about their standards.[5] Thus, even educational institutions are subject to pressures that create lapses in integrity.

Issues related to fairness and honesty in business may arise because business is sometimes viewed as a "game" played by its own set of rules rather than those of society. Author Eric Beversluis suggests that unfairness is a problem because people often reason along the following lines:

1. Business relationships are governed by their own rules, which, in a market society, involve competition, profit maximization, and personal advancement within the organization.

2. Business can therefore be considered a game people play, comparable to competitive sports such as basketball or boxing.

3. Ordinary rules and morality do not hold in games like basketball or boxing. (What if a basketball player did unto others as he would have them do unto him? What if a boxer decided it was wrong to try to injure another person?)

4. Logically, then, if business is a game like basketball or boxing, ordinary ethical rules do not apply.[6]

Such reasoning leads some to conclude that all's fair in love and war, sports and business. Such thinking may have spawned a whole shelf of books comparing business to warfare—consider Harvey Mackay's *Swim with the Sharks* and Jay Conrad Levinson's *Guerrilla Marketing*. The common theme of these books is that surprise attacks, guerrilla warfare, and other warlike tactics are necessary to win the battle for consumers' dollars. This business-as-war mentality may foster the idea that fairness and honesty are not necessary in business.

Many of us would argue, however, that businesses, nonprofits, and other organizations are not involved in a game like basketball or boxing. Because people are not economically self-sufficient, they cannot withdraw from the game of business. Therefore, organizational integrity must not only make clear what rules apply in the "game of work" but must also develop rules appropriate to the nonvoluntary nature of participation in the game.[7]

Communications

Ethical and legal issues in communications relate to promotional messages and information about product content, product safety, pollution, employee work conditions, and other situations. False or misleading promotions can destroy customers' trust in an organization and therefore are a key issue in communications. Abuses in communications range from exaggerated claims and concealed facts to outright lying, and may occur in a variety of departments and functional areas. Such abuses can turn ethical issues into legal ones. For example, the Federal Trade Commission has filed a complaint regarding Exxon's claim that its high-octane gasoline makes engines cleaner and reduces maintenance costs. The FTC believes Exxon's claim is misleading, and the agency has challenged the firm to substantiate its claims or stop making them.[8]

Communications can also mislead by concealing facts within a message. When the Philip Morris Companies launched the new Merit brand cigarette in the 1970s, for example, it was touted as a low-tar cigarette. Many consumers naturally assumed that meant that Merit also had lower nicotine levels. Not until 1995, when the Food and Drug Administration began to scrutinize nicotine as a drug, was it brought to light that there is not necessarily a direct relationship between tar and nicotine. Modern agricultural and filter advances have helped cigarette makers lower the tar content while retaining taste and nicotine levels.[9] Such examples create ethical and legal issues because the communicated messages do not include all the facts consumers need to make good purchasing decisions. They may frustrate and anger customers, who feel that they have been deceived. In addition, they damage the seller's credibility and reputation.

Another communications issue relates to the use of ambiguous statements that require the viewer, reader, or listener to infer the advertiser's intended message. For example advertising for a product may claim that it "helps prevent" this and "helps fight" that, or "helps make you feel" sexy-younger-wonderful-or-whatever-consumers-want-to-hear. Such statements are inherently vague and enable the advertiser to deny any intent to deceive.[10] Consumers may view such advertisements as unscrupulous because they fail to communicate all the information needed to make a good purchasing decision or because they deceive the consumer outright.

Conflict of Interest

To avoid conflicts of interest, employees must be able to separate their private interests from their work responsibilities and relationships. In the United States and Canada, it is generally accepted that employees should not accept bribes, kickbacks, personal payments, gifts, or special favors from others who hope to influence the outcome of a decision. However, bribery is an accepted way of doing business in many countries. One defense industry firm, for example, faced fines of up to $20 million after admitting to making questionable payments of more than $30 million in Egypt. In this case executives apparently used phony documents to hide bribes of Egyptian officials, which were classified as "termination" or "other" fees. A number of other defense contractors have agreed to multimillion dollar settlements for their activities in Egypt, Taiwan, and the Middle East, with many company and government employees losing their jobs as well. When a government official accepts a bribe, it is usually from a business that seeks some favor, perhaps a chance to influence legislation that affects it. Giving bribes to legislators or public officials, then, is an organizational integrity issue.

Conflicts of interest can arise in any type of organization. Louisiana state law enforcement agencies, for example, have come under fire for policies that create the opportunity for such conflicts. In Louisiana, some police departments receive financial rewards for seizing "drug-related" possessions (e.g., cars, jewelry, cash) during arrests. Sixty percent of the financial value of the possessions is returned to the arresting department to use for salary increases and other programs. However, this policy seems to have made some officers more interested in seizing possessions than fighting crime. Many citizens were arrested for little reason and their possessions confiscated, and they often had little legal recourse to fight back.[11] This law therefore created a conflict between public safety and the officers' and departments' focus on financial gain. Conflicts of interest are of particular concern when they create power imbalances, stifle fair competition, or, at worst, endanger the rights and safety of others.

Relating Ethical and Legal Issues to Participants and Functional Areas of Organizations

To help you further evaluate legal and ethical issues, we'll examine the major players and functions of organizations from which integrity questions may arise. The players, obviously, are customers and the public, owners/shareholders/directors, and employees; management, marketing, and finance and accounting are three major functions of most firms.

Customers and the Public

Obviously, the major role of any organization is to satisfy customers. To do so, companies must determine what their customers and other stakeholders want and need, and then create products that will satisfy those wants and needs. Most firms also strive to build long-term relationships with customers. These relationships come through careful planning, follow-up, and a general concern for both company and customer welfare. Many times, this concern also extends to the general public, including a focus on noncustomers or prospective customers.

In attempting to satisfy customers, your organization must consider not only consumers' immediate needs but also their long-term desires. For example, although people want efficient, low-cost energy to power their homes and automobiles, they do not want energy production to pollute the air and water, kill wildlife, or cause disease and birth defects in children. Consumers also expect nutritious food in large quantities at low prices and in convenient form, but they do not want food producers to injure or kill valued wildlife in the process. When consumers learned that dolphins were often killed in the process of catching tuna, many boycotted tuna producers to protest, and the tuna producers responded by developing "dolphin-safe" tuna products. Similarly, several large cosmetics companies have stopped testing cosmetics on animals in response to public outcry. Organizations in general want to satisfy their customers and other publics and are usually willing to make requested changes in order to appease concerned individuals and avoid losses from boycotts and negative publicity.

In the last several years, however, environmental dilemmas have focused the public's attention and demonstrated the tenuous nature of ethics and social responsibility in business. For example, should acres of forest land be preserved to save the rare spotted owl from extinction? If so, then families in such small towns as Port Angeles and Forks, Washington, would lose their jobs and whole communities might disappear because these communities derive the majority of their livelihood from the forestry industry. A picture drawn by a seven-year-old sums up the issue, "An owl needs 2,000 acres to live, why can't I have room to live?"[12] What kind of response to these conflicting priorities will appease concerned consumers and avert negative publicity? Businesspeople and other professionals are often faced with such ethical dilemmas, and there clearly are no easy answers.

Owners/Shareholders/Directors

Owners and shareholders who fail to understand the ethical issues that their customers and society consider important may pay for their lack of understanding in lost sales. Directors of an organization should also educate themselves about relevant legal and ethical issues. For example, after Caremark International was fined $250 million for making illegal payments to doctors as an incentive to prescribe Caremark services, the firm's shareholders sued the company's directors for failing to properly supervise employees. A judge ruled that the directors had exercised due diligence in ensuring legal and ethical compliance because they had named a senior executive as compliance officer, established a code of ethics, and set up an internal auditing system. Although this decision may effectively set a "low standard" for compliance programs that exist in name only, it highlights the responsibility of corporate and nonprofit directors in promoting organizational integrity.[13] Thus, the action or inaction by directors, shareholders, and owners has a direct bearing on organizational integrity.

Employees

Employees who are committed to organizational integrity try to maintain confidentiality in relationships, meet obligations and responsibilities, and avoid putting undue pressure on others that might encourage them to behave unethically or illegally. However, employees may have to make decisions about assignments that they perceive as unethical. For example, Jeffrey Wigand, a former executive at Brown & Williamson Tobacco Corporation and holder of a doctorate in endocrinology and biochemistry, believed that he could make a safer cigarette. However, Wigand alleges that Brown & Williamson disagreed with his research, canceling support of his department's efforts and eventually firing him. He believes that the company is hiding the truth about cigarettes from the public.[14]

Bosses also may not want employees to tell them the truth, especially if it would be detrimental to a superior or the company. Consider the case of Margaret Goodearl and Ruth Aldred, who worked as supervisors in Hughes Aircraft Company's electronics manufacturing division. They accused their employer of falsifying quality-control tests on certain electronic circuits used in tanks, fighters, and missile-guidance systems, which may have threatened the reliability of crucial military hardware. Goodearl and Aldred say the company and some of their coworkers retaliated against them after they agreed to cooperate with federal investigators. Hughes recently settled a lawsuit brought by the whistleblowers for $4.5 million, several years after paying $3.5 million in criminal penalties for the same offenses.[15]

Sabotage is another employee issue that companies must deal with occasionally. Employee sabotage is usually a one-time occurrence and the work of an individual who believes that a promotion or raise was unfairly denied. Michael Lauffenburger, a programmer at General Dynamics, became so disgruntled after not being promoted that he created a logic bomb (a computer program that would destroy the company's parts program and then destroy itself). Lauffenburger quit several months before the program was to be activated and planned to act as a consultant to General Dynamics to rebuild the computer program.[16] Unlike sabotage, employee theft may be an ongoing, routine occurrence. Marita Juse, alias Tammy Gonzalez, did wire transfers for Pinkerton Security Investigation Services' accounting department. One day she was delegated to cancel a former superior's approval code, which she instead appropriated for her own use. Over the next two years, Juse siphoned off more than $1 million; she was sentenced to twenty-seven months in prison.[17] Such theft costs U.S. companies hundreds of millions of dollars every year.

Management

Managers of all organizations have both an ethical and a legal responsibility to manage their firms in the interest of various constituents—owners and stockholders, employees, and society. Several ethical issues relate to managers' obligations to owners, especially in the area of corporate takeovers, mergers, and leveraged buyouts. When a corporation faces the prospect of being bought or taken over, the managers' duties to stockholders may conflict with their own personal interests and objectives (job security, income, and power), and their loyalty to the firm and to stockholders. A management team may even attempt to block a takeover that would benefit shareholders but reduce management's power and perhaps jeopardize their jobs.

Because they guide employees and direct activities, managers directly influence the ethical and legal issues that evolve within an organization. Employees' behaviors and attitudes toward ethical and legal issues are influenced by their superiors. Thus, managers must balance the organization's objectives with responsibilities to subordinates. Managers are often concerned about issues related to employee discipline, discrimination, health and safety, privacy, employee benefits, drug and alcohol abuse in the workplace, the environmental impact of the organization, codes of ethics and self-governance, relations with local communities, plant closings, and layoffs. When such issues are not addressed, employees and communities often react adversely. For example, workers at Rockwell International's Denver plant sued the company for $30 million because they were not given adequate notice of their plant's closing.[18]

Marketing

Ethical and legal issues in marketing may relate to product safety concerns, advertising, selling practices, pricing, or distribution relationships. Product-related ethical issues often arise when marketers fail to disclose risks associated with the product or information regarding the function, value, or use of the product. Compaq Computer, for example, filed suit against Packard Bell, accusing its rival of marketing computers with used parts as new and even altering serial numbers on components to hide their prior use. Although some manufacturers recycle good parts from returned PCs into new machines, Compaq, IBM, and other major manufacturers do not. Compaq took the issue to court in an effort "to level the playing field and get everyone to play by the same rules," says one research consultant.[19]

One of the most widely publicized product safety issues relates to silicon breast implants, which may have contributed to health problems in thousands of women. Faced with a class-action lawsuit, several producers of silicone-gel implants have tentatively agreed to a $4.2 billion global settlement to compensate women who claim they have been harmed by the implants. The implant case has brought several scandals to light. For example, former Dow Chemical general counsel Wayne M. Hancock may have known as early as May 1993 that affidavits concerning the implants were in error, yet he did not correct them.[20]

Price can also create issues. For instance, Johnson & Johnson's cancer drug, Ergamisol, costs a patient $1,250 to $1,500 for one year's supply. The ethical issue derives from the fact that Ergamisol is the same 30-year-old drug Levamisole that J&J markets as a sheep dewormer. The company contends that Ergamisol's price reflects the costs of research to find the drug's cancer-treating properties. Opponents have a different view. Cancer expert and physician Charles G. Moertel says, "To find a new use for an old drug is a sort of windfall that doesn't justify a price surge. Just because aspirin was found to improve your risk of heart attack should you charge more?"[21]

Other issues concern the promotion and distribution of messages to questionable target markets. For example, the *Weekly Reader,* a newsletter targeted at elementary school children, was found to have disseminated pro-tobacco-industry views and positive images of Joe Camel—the cartoon character created to promote Camel cigarettes—in numerous issues. The newsletter is owned by a subsidiary of Kohlberg Kravis Roberts, which until recently was the largest shareholder of RJR Nabisco, the marketer of Camel and other brands of cigarettes. Children's and health advocates say that by not balancing such articles with more information about the hazards of smoking, the articles may have reinforced the tobacco industry's promotion and encouraged children to smoke.[22] Some people may question whether RJR Nabisco has taken unfair advantage of its association with the *Weekly Reader* to promote its product inappropriately at children. This could also be viewed as a distribution issue in that RJR Nabisco used the *Weekly Reader* channel to reach youngsters.

Finance and Accounting

The functions of finance and accounting are replete with opportunities to engage in questionable practices. Integrity issues in finance usually center on how financial resources are acquired and used and how an organization's financial position is reported. Financial documents provide important information on which investors and others base decisions that may involve millions of dollars. If those documents contain inaccurate information, whether intentionally or not, lawsuits and criminal penalties may result.

A recent case shows how people responsible for huge corporations can succumb to the opportunity to engage in misconduct. Michael I. Monus, former CEO of Phar-Mor Inc., a discount retail chain, and Patrick Finn, Phar-Mor's chief financial officer, were charged with embezzling at least $10 million. "Cooked books" overstated company earnings by $340 million and inflated inventory by $175 million. The two men were fired, and Phar-Mor went into bankruptcy. Monus was eventually convicted of defrauding eighteen banks in connection with a $600 million line of credit, eleven insurance companies of $155 million in senior secured notes, and London-based National Westminster Bank PLC of a $112 million private stock placement. Under current sentencing guidelines, Monus faces up to 1,246 years in prison and $34 million in fines for fraud, embezzlement, conspiracy, and filing false income returns.[23]

Accountants who report and/or audit financial data face their own set of pressures. The field of accounting has changed dramatically over the last decade. The profession used to have a club mentality: certified public accountants (CPAs) were not concerned about competition. Now CPAs advertise their skills in an increasingly competitive environment in which overall billable hours have significantly decreased because of technological advances. In addition to competition, accountants face pressures related to time, reduced fees, client requests for altered opinions or for lower tax payments, complex rules and regulations, data overload, contingency fees, and commissions. An accountant's life is filled with rules and data that have to be interpreted correctly. As a result, accountants must abide by a strict code of ethics, which defines their responsibilities to their clients and the public interest. These codes, which are part of state certifications and national associations, usually address the concepts of integrity, objectivity, independence, and due care.

Because accountants are guided by such standards, it would be reasonable to assume that they have a fairly clear understanding of ethics and legal issues, but apparently that is not the case. The American Institute of Certified Public Accountants (AICPA) recently added a new requirement to its code: If a company's financial statements are "materially misstated," the accountant should consider reporting the problem to his or her superior. Going along with any type of cover-up could result in a loss of license. However, Robert C. Reeves, Jr., says he was fired for reporting such misstatements at Aetna Life & Casualty Co. Aetna denies the allegation and says Reeves' job was eliminated as part of a "reduction in staff." A court will decide the issue.[24]

Another financial issue relates to whether banks should be held responsible for knowing whether large cash deposits are being "laundered" to hide the depositor's involvement in drug trafficking. Society's need to enforce drug-related laws may conflict with banks' desires to maintain their customers' confidentiality. Although U.S. banks have tightened controls, unethical and illegal practitioners have sidestepped banks by using wire transfers. Robert Hirsch, a banking and entertainment attorney, favored this type of money-laundering method until he received death threats from the Cali cocaine cartel unless he turned over $425,000. When CIA agents helped him out, he did not realize that they also knew that he had stolen $2.5 million from members of the cartel.[25]

RECOGNIZING AN ETHICAL ISSUE

Although we have described a number of relationships and situations that may create ethical and legal issues, it can be difficult to recognize specific issues in practice. To better understand the issues that may arise in your organization, we suggest developing a matrix that uses the three categories and/or major participants and business functions. Table 2-1 provides an example of situations an organization may face.

TABLE 2-1
Potential Ethical and Legal Issues in the Workplace

	Conflict of Interest	Communications
Customers	• Paying bribes to government officials in order to secure contracts • Reducing a product's safety features in order to lower manufacturing costs	• Making excessive claims about product performance • Promising to deliver by a certain date, while knowing the shipment will be two weeks late
Employees	• Using quotas that encourage salespeople to place personal interests over customer needs • Requiring employees to work long hours and weekends without additional compensation	• Monitoring employees' electronic and voice mail communications • Failing to educate employees of health and safety risks on the job

One way to determine whether a specific behavior or situation has an ethical or legal component is to ask other individuals in your organization how they feel about it and whether they approve. Table 2-2 lists ten warning signs of ethical issues: Employees who use or hear these phrases may be facing a decision that requires guidance from management and organizational policy. Another way is to determine whether your firm has adopted specific policies on the activity. An activity that is legal, approved of by most members of your organization, and customary in your industry is probably acceptable. An issue, activity, or situation that can withstand open discussion between many groups, both in and outside the organization, and survive untarnished probably does not pose ethical problems. Failure to discuss legal issues and acknowledge ethical issues is a great danger in any organization, particularly if your "business" is treated as a game in which ordinary rules of fairness do not apply. Sometimes people who take this view do things that are not only unethical but also illegal in order to maximize their own position or boost the profits or goals of the organization.

TABLE 2-2
Ten Warning Signs of Possible Ethical and Legal Issues and Conflict

1. "Everybody does it."
2. "No one is going to get hurt."
3. "Boys will be boys."
4. "No one will ever miss it."
5. "Don't be such a prude."
6. "Let's keep this one between us."
7. "Just this once."
8. "Look the other way."
9. "They had it coming to them anyway."
10. "It could be a real sweet deal if you ..."

Source: Adapted from *Ethics in Our Work Place*, (Oakbrook, IL: Waste Management, Inc., 1992).

Because laws, regulations, and societal expectations are subject to change, all organizations need mechanisms for evaluating and responding to a dynamic legal and ethical environment. As part of its corporate compliance program, TECO Energy Inc. conducts periodic reviews of the ethical and legal issues that should be addressed by its "Standards of Integrity" effort. The company's tools for raising employees' awareness of legal and ethical issues include mandatory legal seminars, ethics training, and periodic communications to specific departments and functions.[26] Learning to recognize the potential risk areas and issues that your organization faces is a first step in creating a successful integrity effort. As with any strategic initiative, it begins with analyzing relevant issues and then designing appropriate responses and plans. Once an employee recognizes that an ethical or legal issue exists and can openly discuss it with others, he or she has begun the decision-making process we'll look at in Chapter 3. The remaining chapters will help you in evaluating and resolving ethical dilemmas.

INTEGRITY MANAGER CHECKLIST

The following questions will assess your organization's ability to effectively manage ethical and legal issues. A high number of affirmative responses indicates a focused effort on both understanding and responding to issues in the workplace.

YES   NO

❏   ❏   Does your organization have methods for detecting ethical concerns within the organization?

❏   ❏   Does your organization have methods for detecting ethical concerns externally with suppliers and customers?

❏   ❏   Do individuals in your organization understand the legal issues that affect their work decisions?

❏   ❏   Is there open communication between superiors and subordinates to discuss ethical dilemmas and conflicts?

❏   ❏   Have there been instances where employees have received advice on how to improve ethical behavior?

❏   ❏   Have there been instances where employees were disciplined for committing unethical or illegal acts?

❏   ❏   Does your firm have specific policies on the legal and ethical dilemmas that are common in your industry?

CHAPTER THREE

UNDERSTANDING DECISION MAKING IN THE WORKPLACE

Integrity is our collective personal responsibility. And a dedication to quality characterizes our professional relationships.

– Computer Sciences Corporation, *CSC Culture*, found at www.csc.com

In 1989, Mark Whitacre went to work at Archer-Daniels-Midland Company (ADM) as head of its new biochemical products division. While struggling to get a lysine-production unit up and running, Whitacre contends that he encountered a number of difficult issues, including finding a possible saboteur, being asked to participate in the formation of a "cooperative association" with ADM's competitors, and being asked to lie to the FBI about ADM's activities. Instead of lying to the FBI, Whitacre voiced his concerns about possible price fixing in the lysine industry. Thus began Mark Whitacre's role as mole and whistleblower, a role which eventually led to ADM pleading guilty to price-fixing charges and paying a record fine of $100 million. While Whitacre continues to maintain that he believes he did the right thing in exposing ADM's misconduct, it appears his hands are not entirely clean: ADM has accused him of stealing millions of dollars from the company.' Why did Mark Whitacre choose to blow the whistle on ADM? Did he steal money from his employer even while exposing ADM's misconduct, and if so why did he make that decision?

To improve integrity within your organization, it is helpful to consider this question of why and how people make ethical and legal decisions. Too often it has been assumed that people make tough decisions within an organization in the same way they resolve difficult issues in their personal lives. Within the context of organizations, however, few of us have the freedom to decide ethical issues independently of workplace pressures. Philosophers, social scientists, and other academics have attempted to explain the ethical decision-making process in business by examining these pressures, including the influence of coworkers and organizational culture, as well as individual factors, such as personal moral philosophy. In this chapter, we have synthesized our current knowledge of legal and ethical decision making in the workplace.[2]

Figure 3-1 illustrates our model of decision making, which indicates that the perceived intensity of ethical and legal issues, individual factors—such as moral development and personal moral philosophy—and organizational factors—including organizational culture and coworkers—influence whether a person will make an unethical or illegal decision at work. While it is impossible to describe precisely how or why an individual or a work group might make these decisions, we can generalize about average or typical behavior patterns within organizations.

FIGURE 3-1
Our Model for Understanding Ethical Decision Making in the Workplace

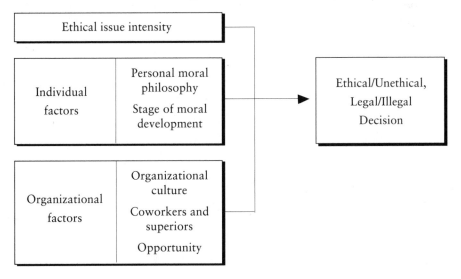

This model is practical because it describes the elements of the decision-making process over which your organization has control.

ETHICAL ISSUE INTENSITY

One of the first factors to influence the decision-making process is how important or relevant a decision maker perceives an issue to be—i.e., the intensity of the issue.[3] The intensity of a particular issue is likely to vary over time and among individuals and is influenced by the values, beliefs, needs, and perceptions of the decision maker; the special characteristics of the situation; and the personal pressures weighing on the decision. All the other factors we will explore in this chapter, including personal moral development and philosophy, organizational culture, and coworkers, determine why different people perceive issues with varying intensity.[4] Unless individuals in an organization share some common concerns about specific ethical issues, the stage is set for conflict. Ethical issue intensity reflects the sensitivity of the individual, work group, or organization and triggers the ethical decision-making process.

Management can influence ethical issue intensity through rewards and punishments, codes of conduct, and organizational values. In other words, managers can affect the perceived importance of an ethical issue through positive and/or negative incentives.[5] If management fails to identify and educate employees about problem areas, these issues may not reach the critical awareness level of some employees. New employees who lack experience in a particular industry, for example, may have trouble identifying both ethical and legal issues. Employees therefore need to be trained on how the organization wants specific ethical issues handled. Identifying ethical issues that employees might encounter is a significant step in developing employees' ability to make decisions that enhance organizational integrity.

Many ethical issues are identified by industry groups or through general information in newspapers and other media. For example, discrimination based on race, sex, or age is considered an important issue in most firms and certainly by our society. Discrimination often stems from negative attitudes toward a particular group. For example, several studies have revealed that African-Americans, particularly women, pay significantly higher prices for new cars than do whites.[6] Employees of auto dealers should be made aware that price differences based on race are an ethical issue with serious consequences for the firm and society.

The experiences of Denny's restaurant chain reinforce the idea that raising the ethical intensity of an issue via communication with and education of employees is critical to ethical compliance. Denny's was sued on the grounds of discrimination several times in the 1990s. One litigant, Donnette Stahnke, an African-American, claimed that she was passed over in favor of white applicants for jobs at a Denny's restaurant. Before bringing suit, her lawyer sent three black and three white "applicants" to the restaurant. The white women were all offered jobs, but the black women were not, even though they had slightly better credentials. Denny's paid $45.7 million in 1994 to settle a class-action lawsuit brought by black customers who said that they were ignored or treated rudely by Denny's workers.[7] It is almost impossible for widespread discrimination and mistreatment to occur without top management, as well as supervisory management, condoning, or at least ignoring the behavior. In the Denny's case, management needed to develop an effective communication and compliance system to identify discrimination as a major ethical issue in its restaurants. All employees should understand both the ethical and legal consequences of discrimination.

To comply with new federal regulations that hold both organizations *and* their employees responsible for misconduct, organizations must assess areas of ethical and legal risk that are, in reality, ethical issues. When firms communicate to employees that certain issues are important, the intensity of the issues is elevated. The more employees appreciate the importance of an issue, the less likely they are to engage in questionable behavior associated with the issue.[8] Therefore, ethical issue intensity should be considered a key factor in the decision-making process because there are many opportunities for the organization to influence and educate employees on the importance of specific issues.

INDIVIDUAL FACTORS

Perhaps one of the greatest challenges facing the study of organizational integrity involves the role of individuals and their values. Although most of us would like to place the primary responsibility for decisions with individuals, years of research point to the primacy of organizational factors in determining integrity at work. However, individual factors are obviously important in the evaluation and resolution of ethical issues, although they are just one element of ethical decision making at work, as we shall see later. Two significant factors in workplace integrity are an individual's personal moral philosophy and stage of moral development.

Personal Moral Philosophy

Ethical conflict occurs when people encounter situations that they cannot easily control or resolve. In such situations, people tend to base their decisions on their own principles of right or wrong and act accordingly in their daily lives. Moral philosophies—the principles or rules that individuals use to decide what is right or wrong—are often cited to justify decisions or explain behavior. People learn these principles and rules through socialization by family members, social groups, religion, and formal education. At least two major types of moral philosophy are associated with workplace decisions: utilitarianism and formalized rules and rights.

Utilitarianism is concerned with maximizing the greatest good for the greatest number of people. Utilitarians judge an action or decision by the consequences for everyone affected. In other words, in a situation with an ethical component, utilitarians compare all possible options and choose the one that promises the best results for all concerned. A manager who chooses to raise product prices in order to maintain the survival of her company and preserve her employees' jobs, which in turn contributes to the well-being of the local community, is probably applying a utilitarian philosophy to the decision-making process.

In contrast, a rights- or rules-oriented philosophy focuses on the intentions associated with a particular behavior and on the rights of the individual. This philosophy, sometimes called ethical formalism, develops specific standards of behavior by determining whether an action can be taken consistently as a general rule, without considering alternative results.[9] People who strive to live by the Golden Rule—do unto others as you would have them do unto you—exemplify the rules and rights philosophy. This philosophy judges an action or decision on the basis of whether it infringes on individual rights or universal rules.

An executive who decides that a product should not be marketed because there is a *small* chance it may cause harm to consumers is probably an ethical formalist. His "rule" states that companies should not knowingly sell potentially harmful products.

There is no universal agreement on the correct moral philosophy to use in resolving ethical and legal issues in the workplace. Moreover, research suggests that employees may apply different moral philosophies in different decision situations. Each philosophy could result in a different decision in an ethical dilemma. And, depending on the situation, people may even change their value structure or moral philosophy when making decisions. We've probably all made decisions under pressure that we later felt were less than acceptable. In such instances, we may have experienced pressure to go against our "natural" tendency; instead, we relied on another moral stance that seemed appropriate for the specific time and place.

Stage of Moral Development

One reason people may change their moral philosophy has been proposed by psychologist Lawrence Kohlberg, who suggested that people progress through stages in their development of moral reasoning. Kohlberg contends that different people make different decisions when confronted with similar ethical situations because they are at different stages of what he called cognitive moral development.[10] He believes that people progress through the following three stages:

1. *The preconventional stage.* People in this stage of moral development focus on individual needs and desires. They define right as literal obedience to rules and authority and respond to rules and labels of "good" and "bad" in terms of the physical power of those who determine such rules. As people progress through this stage, they rely less on specific rules or authority figures and evaluate behavior on the basis of its fairness to themselves.

2. *The conventional stage.* In the conventional stage of moral development, people focus on group-centered values and conforming to expectations. They are still motivated by obedience to rules, but they also consider the well-being of others. As they progress through

this stage, individuals determine what is right by considering their duty to society, not just to other specific people. Duty, respect for authority, and maintaining social order become the focal points, and life is valued in terms of its place in society.

3. *The principled stage.* In the principled stage of moral development, people are concerned with upholding the basic rights, values, and rules of society. They feel a sense of obligation, a "social contract," to other groups and recognize that in some cases legal and moral points of view may conflict. An individual who reaches this highest level of moral development believes that right is determined by universal ethical principles that everyone should follow. He or she may be more concerned with social ethical issues and not rely on the organization for ethical direction.[11]

We should note that there is some spillover effect among these stages, and that cognitive moral development can be viewed as more of a continuum.

Although Kohlberg did not specifically apply his theory of cognitive moral development to organizations, we find it helpful in explaining how employees may reason when confronted with a dilemma. Kohlberg's theory suggests that people may change their moral beliefs and behavior as they gain education and experience in resolving conflicts, which helps accelerate their progress along the moral development continuum. A survey by the Ethics Resource Center provides some

TABLE 3-1
Changes in Career Business Ethics over Time

In a survey of 4,000 employees in a variety of U.S. industries, responses to the question, "Has your business ethics changed during the course of your career"?

Greatly improved	12%
Modestly improved	37%
Not changed	43%
Modestly declined	6%
Greatly declined	0.6%

Source: Rebecca Goodell, *Ethics in American Business: Policies, Programs, and Perceptions* (1994), 15. Permission provided courtesy of the Ethics Resource Center, 1747 Pennsylvania Avenue NW, Suite 400, Washington, D.C. 20005.

evidence that this indeed occurs. Nearly half (49 percent) of the 4,000 individuals surveyed believed that their business ethics had improved over the course of their careers (see Table 3-1). More than one-third (34 percent) thought their business ethics had improved because of their personal ethics. Surprisingly, nearly one in eight (13 percent) believed that their personal ethics had improved because of their business ethics.[12] For this reason, some organizations are using educational training programs designed to help employees progress to higher levels of moral reasoning.

An obvious question that arises here is whether moral philosophy and moral development can predict ethical behavior in business and other organizations. A study we conducted found that only 15 percent of a sample of businesspersons maintained the same moral philosophy across both work and nonwork ethical decision-making situations. One explanation may be that cognitive moral development issues that relate to a person's nonwork experiences, home, and family situations are not the most significant factors in resolving ethical issues within the organization. In fact, we have found that the ethics and values of the individual's immediate work group, rather than his or her moral development, may be the most important consideration in determining conduct in organizations. Nevertheless, most experts agree that a person's stage of moral development and personal moral philosophy play a role in how values and actions are shaped in the workplace. This may be especially true for top managers, who usually set the formal values of a firm. However, the informal use of these values and expectations plays a major role in the daily decisions that employees make. Many of these informal rules comprise the organization's "working" integrity.

ORGANIZATIONAL FACTORS

Although individuals must make ethical and legal choices at work, it is also true that they often make these decisions in committees, group meetings, and through discussion with colleagues. Decisions in the workplace are guided by the organization's culture and the influence of others—coworkers, superiors, subordinates—so let's take a closer look at these factors.

Organizational Culture

Organizations, like societies, have cultures that include a set of values, beliefs, goals, norms, and ways to solve problems that employees share. As time passes, an organization comes to be seen as a living organism, with a mind and will of its own. For example, the corporate culture at American Express Company stresses that employees help customers out of difficult situations whenever possible. This attitude is reinforced (and advertised) through numerous company legends of employees who have gone above and beyond the call of duty to help customers. This strong tradition of customer loyalty might encourage an American Express employee to take unorthodox steps to help a customer who encounters a problem while traveling overseas. Such strong traditions and values have become a driving force in many companies, including McDonald's Corp., IBM, The Procter & Gamble Co., Hershey Foods, and the Walt Disney Company. The Walt Disney Company even requires all new employees to take a course in the traditions and history of Disneyland and Walt Disney to socialize them into the company's culture.

Although most organizational cultures reinforce integrity, some support unethical decisions. If a company derives most of its profits from unethical or illegal activities, then individuals who join this organization will have a hard time surviving unless they too participate in these activities. Consider, for example, companies that market devices which decode, or pirate, satellite television signals. Such piracy undercuts the proprietary interests of companies such as Direct TV, which provide satellites for their customers to obtain television programming reception for a fee. Viewers can avoid these fees by plugging one of these illegal decoding devices into the back of a satellite receiver. The companies that market these illegal decoders have developed a corporate scheme to steal satellite television signals.[13] Although this is an extreme example of a corrupt corporate culture, the important point is that employees of such organizations are, by virtue of their employment, actively buying into a climate of deception and dishonesty. The ethical climate of such companies is clearly based on pure profit considerations, not the rights of others.

The ethical climate of an organization is a significant element of organizational culture. Whereas a firm's overall culture establishes ideals that guide a wide range of behaviors for members of the organization, its ethical climate focuses specifically on issues of right and wrong. We think of the ethical climate as the organization's character or conscience. Codes of conduct and ethics policies, top management's actions on ethical issues, the values and moral development and philosophies of coworkers, and the opportunity for misconduct all contribute to an organization's ethical climate. In fact, the ethical climate actually determines whether or not certain issues are perceived as having an ethical component. From our example on the piracy of television signals, it is easy to imagine how some companies would react to the mere suggestion of marketing such a device. In a firm with a strong ethical climate, there would be little consideration of selling a device with the primary purpose of aiding illegal activity. This climate would not support such a strategic business alternative. The recognition of ethical issues and the generation of alternatives to resolve them are manifestations of ethical climate.

Organizations can manage their culture and ethical climate by trying to hire employees whose values match their own. Some firms even measure potential employees' values during the hiring process and strive to choose individuals who "fit" within the ethical climate rather than those whose beliefs and values differ significantly. A poor "fit" can have very expensive ramifications for both organizations and employees. Beyond the potential for misconduct, a poor employee-organization ethical fit usually results in low job satisfaction, decreased performance, and higher turnover.[14] Most people want to make a difference with their work, and they look for organizations that will allow them to achieve their personal goals and purpose.[15]

The Influence of Coworkers and Superiors

Just as employees look for certain types of employers, they are also particular about the people with whom they work. Managers and coworkers within an organization help people deal with unfamiliar tasks and provide advice and information in both formal and informal contexts on a daily basis. A manager, for example, may provide direction regarding certain activities to be performed on the job. Coworkers offer help in the form of discussions over lunch or when the boss is away. In fact, you often hear new or younger employees discussing some fear about approaching "the boss" on a tough issue. Thus, the role of informal culture cannot be underestimated. Numerous studies conducted over the years confirm that such significant others have more impact on a worker's daily decisions than any other factor.

Obedience to authority can also explain why many people resolve workplace issues by following the directives of a superior. (Remember that Kohlberg believed that obedience to authority is the foundation stage in the development of moral reasoning.) In a company that emphasizes respect for superiors, for example, an employee may feel obligated to carry out the orders of a superior even if those orders conflict with the employee's values of right and wrong. Later, if a decision is judged to have been wrong, the employee is likely to say, "I was only carrying out orders," or "My boss told me to do it this way."

Superiors can also have a negative effect on conduct by setting a bad example or failing to supervise subordinates. When authorities discovered that former Kidder Peabody & Co. bond trader Joseph Jett had allegedly invented $350 million in phony bond profits to inflate his bonus and cover up $100 million in losses, Jett's supervisors, Edward Cerullo and Melvin Mullin, were charged with failing to supervise him. Mullin said that he did nothing wrong in failing to supervise Jett. Cerullo settled a securities-fraud charge, agreeing to a one-year suspension from acting as a supervisor in the securities industry and paying a fine of $50,000. However, he did not admit wrongdoing.[16] Many supervisors look the other way and do not want to deal with the conflict and other risks associated with handling misconduct.

Employees also learn ethical or unethical conduct from close colleagues and others with whom they interact regularly. Consequently, a decision maker who associates with others who behave unethically will be more likely to behave unethically as well. In the work group environment, employees may be subject to the phenomenon of "groupthink," where they go along with group decisions even when those decisions run counter to their own values. They may take refuge in the notion of "safety in numbers" when everyone else appears to back a particular decision. We believe that peers can even change a person's original value system. This value change, whether temporary or permanent, appears to be greater when the colleague is a superior, especially if the decision maker is new to the firm. So, peer pressure, the bane of many adolescents, rears its head again.

People who strive to control their own decisions and accept responsibility for them are less likely to be swayed by the opinions of others. Such individuals believe they are masters of their own destiny, and that they make things happen rather than react to events. The degree of a person's self-esteem and self-confidence may contribute to the decision either to go along with ethical (or unethical) decisions or to refuse to participate in certain decisions. A worker who has low self-esteem and is dependent on others may go along with a scheme that results in a questionable activity. When confronted with the misconduct, the employee may argue that she was just doing her job. Conversely, a worker with high self-esteem and a feeling of competence may rely more on his values and, whether right or wrong, will take responsibility for decisions. This person will be less likely to depend on others in resolving ethical issues.

Another aspect of work group relationships is the type of stress or conflict that is found in certain departments and professions. We have all worked in organizations where financial pressures, coworker personalities, and the general climate bred great tension and conflict. Because of the nature of their work, some employees face more stress and many more ethical dilemmas than others. Salespeople, for example, are often confronted by customers who imply that they will purchase a product with a little incentive—that is, a bribe—that may violate company policy. Auditors may be asked to report information in such a way that hides discrepancies. A personnel manager may discriminate against a minority when asked, instead, to hire another employee's close friend. Since there is little doubt that decision making is stressful for employees who face such conflicts, the tendency is for stressful situations to increase the likelihood of unethical and perhaps illegal behavior.

Opportunity

Together, organizational culture and the influence of coworkers may foster conditions that limit or permit misconduct. When these conditions provide rewards—be it financial gain, recognition, promotion, or simply the good feeling from a job well done—the opportunity for unethical conduct may be encouraged—or discouraged. For example, a company policy that does not provide for punishment of employees who violate a rule (e.g., not to accept large gifts from clients) provides an opportunity for unethical behavior. Essentially, this lack of policy allows individuals to engage in such behavior without fear of consequences. Thus, organizational policies, processes, and other factors may contribute to the opportunity to act unethically.

Opportunity usually relates to employees' immediate job context—where they work, with whom they work, and the nature of the work. The specific work situation includes the motivational "carrots and sticks" that superiors can use to influence employee behavior. Pay raises, bonuses, and public recognition are carrots, or positive reinforcers, whereas reprimands, pay penalties, demotions, and even firings act as sticks, the negative reinforcers. For example, a salesperson who is publicly recognized and given a large bonus for making a valuable sale that he obtained through unethical tactics will probably be motivated to use unethical sales tactics in the future, even if such behavior goes against his personal value system. And, often, other salespeople may be motivated by these "carrots" of glory and dollars.

Organizations can improve compliance by eliminating the opportunity to engage in misconduct through the establishment of formal codes, policies, and rules that are adequately enforced. This is why many financial organizations, such as banks, savings and loan associations, and securities companies, have developed elaborate sets of rules and procedures to minimize the opportunity for employees to take advantage of their position. In banks, for example, most employees are required to take vacations and to stay out of the bank a certain number of days every year so that they cannot be physically present in the bank to cover up embezzlement or other diversion of funds. This rule prevents the opportunity for inappropriate conduct.

It is important to note that opportunities for misconduct cannot be eliminated without aggressive enforcement of codes and rules. A national jewelry store chain president explained to one of us how he dealt with a bribery incident. His company had an explicit policy barring the acceptance of incentive payments when dealing with suppliers. When the president learned that one of his buyers had accepted a bribe from a supplier, he immediately traveled to the buyer's office and terminated his employment. The president then traveled to the supplier's office and severed that relationship as well. The president's action sent a clear message to both his firm's buyers and salespeople from supplying companies: *Bribery is unacceptable and will not be tolerated.* Such enforcement removes the opportunity to commit other acts that challenge organizational integrity.

The insurance industry has received a great deal of criticism for exaggeration and unscrupulous sales techniques. Met Life, New York Life, Allstate, and Prudential have been investigated by regulators in Florida and other states for allegedly selling life insurance to nurses as "retirement plans." Failing to identify an insurance product as insurance violates consumer protection laws. However, some insurance agents have found that renaming insurance makes it easier to sell. Other agents have resorted to calling themselves "financial advisors." On the other hand, Minnesota Mutual Life has been striving to help the insurance industry steer clear of such scandal and public outrage. The 114-year old firm has an extensive employee-screening process, a consistent corporate value system, and a systematic review process of sales techniques and materials. Minnesota Mutual Life serves as a role model for other insurance companies as it has a system for managing opportunity, organizational relationships, and individual factors within its organization.[17]

USING THE DECISION-MAKING MODEL AS A FOUNDATION FOR WORKPLACE INTEGRITY

Our decision-making model can help prepare you to make informed decisions by offering some insights and knowledge about the factors that typically affect the decision-making process in organizations. One important conclusion that should be drawn from our model is that ethical decision making within an organization does not depend solely on individuals' values and moral philosophies. Employees do not operate in a vacuum, and their decisions are strongly affected by the culture and ethical climate of the firm in which they work, pressures to perform, examples set by their superiors and peers, and opportunities created by the presence or absence of ethics-related policies, in addition to their own moral values and level of moral reasoning. Organizations take on an ethical climate of their own and have a significant influence on integrity among employees and within their industry and community.

Obviously, we cannot tell you *why* a specific individual made a specific decision, such as why Mark Whitacre acted as he did while working at ADM. However, we propose that understanding *how* people typically make ethical decisions in an organization will reveal several avenues for improving decision making. Armed with some knowledge about how the decision process works, you will be better prepared to critically analyze ethical issues and to provide integrity leadership regardless of your role in the organization. Our model sets the stage for developing ethical and legal compliance policies and programs for real impact and effective integrity and leadership. The remaining chapters of this book delve into these areas and provide specific guidance and recommendations that complement our decision-making model.

Integrity Manager Checklist

Does your organization understand the various factors that influence the decision-making process that leads to ethical and legal actions? If you can answer yes to many of these questions, then your firm seems both proactive and forthright in examining workplace integrity.

YES NO

❏ ❏ Does your organization have programs and policies to help employees recognize workplace issues that are ethically and legally sensitive?

❏ ❏ Does your organization's management accept responsibility for ethical and legal decision making on the part of employees and agents?

❏ ❏ Does your firm try to hire employees whose values are consistent with organizational culture and expectations?

❏ ❏ Does your organizational culture value integrity as much as financial performance and profitability?

❏ ❏ Is it easy for new employees to recognize your firm's commitment to ethical and legal decision making?

❏ ❏ Are new employees educated on your organization's history, culture, and other relevant issues?

❏ ❏ In your organization, is there a sense of responsibility among coworkers for maintaining a reputation of integrity?

❏ ❏ Does your organization have mechanisms for helping employees manage work-related stress and conflict?

❏ ❏ Are some employees "getting away" with certain behaviors because they are successfully achieving other organizational goals?

❏ ❏ Is your firm sensitive to changing societal expectations regarding workplace practices?

CHAPTER FOUR

MANAGING ORGANIZATIONAL CULTURE FOR INTEGRITY

*Judge us by what we are doing, not by
what we say we are going to do.*

> – Terry Pritchett, General Motors' Corporate
> Affairs Department, quoted in *Business Ethics*
> 10 (November/December 1996): 5.

Throughout much of the 1990s, Arthur C. Martinez, now CEO of Sears, Roebuck and Co., has been determined to completely reinvent the retail giant on several different levels. From the beginning, Martinez recognized that bringing the company out of its economic doldrums required more than just cutting costs and downsizing; he had to completely transform the retailer's culture. Martinez began by throwing out the company's nearly 30,000 pages of policies and procedures and replacing them with a slim folder outlining employee obligations, company beliefs and values, and a code of business conduct. Martinez divided Sears' ethics initiative into five components: (1) keep it simple; (2) provide broad guidelines and guidance; (3) act decisively with unethical behavior; (4) trust all employees to make the right decisions; and (5) create partnerships with both internal and external stakeholders to establish a mutual set of workplace values. This ethics initiative has been a major component of Sears' economic and cultural turnaround.[1]

Arthur C. Martinez obviously believes, as we do, that culture is a major factor in organizational integrity. Organizational culture—including values, traditions, pressures exerted by coworkers and managers, and policies that are strictly enforced—has a profound effect on whether employees make ethical and legal decisions. Most people want to work for and with organizations that maintain high levels of integrity. Although a high standard of ethics will not necessarily motivate such employees to work harder, it may keep them from altering their own values or making poor decisions in the face of peer pressure, motivation to reach unrealistic financial goals, and other sources of conflict in the workplace.

To create a "good citizen" organization with high levels of integrity and ethics, one that you and your employees will be proud to work for, it is necessary to manage your firm's culture. In this chapter, we therefore focus on how organizational culture—through rewards, leadership, and interpersonal relationships—influences workplace integrity. We will examine the role of culture at several focal points—the development of formal values and expectations for workplace integrity, working to align values with other organizational systems and practices, and understanding how interpersonal relationships affect the informal interpretation of these values. We also provide specific guidance on managing components of culture that both contribute to and detract from integrity.

THE IMPLICATIONS OF
ORGANIZATIONAL CULTURE IN DECISION MAKING

For years, many people associated the New Orleans, Louisiana, Police Department with widespread corruption. This connection was perhaps not unfounded, as an unusual number of police officers and department employees were convicted of crimes ranging from petty theft to murder. In an effort to clean up the department and restore New Orleans' trust in law enforcement, new police superintendent Richard J. Pennington created a "Public Integrity" division and mandated professional ethics training as a major component of the police academy curriculum. These efforts have been praised as worthwhile and necessary for improving the police department's internal operations and public reputation, but much remains to be done. While he has rid the NOPD of many "bad apples," Pennington also understands the influence that policies, management, and coworkers have on the decisions and behaviors that foster integrity in his organization. Essentially, he faces the task of completely transforming an organizational culture that, for many years, tolerated both illegal and unethical behavior.[2]

As we emphasized in the last chapter, organizational integrity is a function of several different dimensions of an organization's system: organizational culture, opportunity, coworkers and management, and the values of the organization's individual members. Corporate values tend to dominate most organizational cultures, particularly in the absence of individual ethical values. Although personal values are involved in ethical decisions, they are just one of the elements that guide the decisions, actions, and policies of organizations. An organization's values, as derived from its procedures and policies, tend to drive it toward certain goals and along certain pathways. Thus the burden of ethical behavior relates to the organization's values and traditions, not just to the individuals who make the decisions and carry them out.[3]

We can expand on the idea of "bad apples" to help explain the relationship between personal values and organizational culture in organizational integrity. The "bad apple" argument—the notion that blame for unethical or illegal behavior rests with a few unsavory individuals—assumes that people are either ethical or unethical, depending on personal moral development, and it implies that organizations can do little to influence ethical behavior. If the bad apple principle is true, then organizations should attempt to identify unethical individuals and avoid hiring them or remove them from the organization.[4]

But what if the barrel is bad? The idea of the "bad barrel" is that something in the barrel poisons otherwise good apples; in other words, the organizational culture poisons otherwise ethical people. This view assumes that people, even seasoned and mature adults, can be influenced by the organizational culture surrounding them, including peers, superiors, and the reward system.[5] The example of the New Orleans Police Department of years past illustrates that organizational culture can contribute to an atmosphere in which people have the opportunity to make questionable decisions, particularly under the influence of peers who themselves engage in misconduct. When organizational members observe coworkers getting away with murder, so to speak, the stage is set for continued misconduct.

ORGANIZATIONAL INFLUENCES ON WORKPLACE INTEGRITY

Because organizational culture has such a profound effect on integrity in the workplace, we need to take a look at some critical elements that help shape it. How organizations reward conduct—whether that conduct is acceptable or not—and how managers lead their firms toward achievement of organizational objectives have a significant impact on decisions in the workplace.

The Influence of Rewards

Even when top management does not formally express desired behaviors and goals, an organizational culture still evolves on its own and, in so doing, begins to informally reflect the goals and values of the organization.[6] If a firm does not formally and explicitly value ethical and legal conduct, then misconduct may be rewarded and sanctioned. In such cases, management should not be surprised when improprieties occur. However, many managers feel they have very little influence on workplace integrity, mainly because they believe that adults' ethical values cannot be changed or influenced.

Although some organizations hesitate to develop written documents outlining their values, the process of doing so will clarify questions regarding formal expectations and provide guidance in tough situations. Consider the history of college athletics. University teams have been known to violate National Collegiate Athletic Association (NCAA) regulations by paying or otherwise compensating college athletes; many of these teams became nationally ranked because they were able to attract the most talented athletes. In some cases, university officials were aware of improprieties but overlooked them because they wanted national recognition and alumni support. The values embedded within these universities contributed to organizational cultures that rewarded illegal and unethical activity in collegiate athletics. And our experience has shown that few universities have their own codes of conduct. In many cases, only the deterrent of NCAA sanctions such as the "death penalty" (not allowing the team to play) have changed the universities' orientation toward integrity.

A university coach once said that he often felt isolated from the rest of the college—with a focus only on winning and keeping the best athletes happy. In a workplace situation such as this, management's sense of the organization's culture may be quite different from the values, ethical beliefs, and daily pressures that actually guide employee behaviors to accomplish goals. So, many questions of integrity arise because of conflicts between the cultural values perceived by management and the ones actually at work in the organization.

Management, for instance, may believe that the culture encourages respect for all coworkers. On the basis of the workplace rewards or sanctions, however, employees may believe that the organization encourages competition among its members. As a result, employees may intentionally or unintentionally sabotage others' work in order to win organizational rewards. Or, the competition may become so intense that employees lose sight of the "big picture" and focus instead on tactical and short-term gains. In this case, there is an obvious misalignment between what managers want for the workplace and the actual rewards and sanctions that ultimately guide employee behaviors.

This discrepancy between the cultural values perceived by management and organizational cultures that actually reward misconduct may be one factor at work in the outbreak of racial and sexual discrimination and harassment charges in recent years. Companies in industries as diverse as food service, retail, industrial manufacturing, professional sales and others have experienced negative publicity and, in some cases, been ordered to pay fines, punitive damages, and back pay to employees who feel they have been discriminated against or worse. A sexual harassment scandal at the U.S. subsidiary of Swedish pharmaceutical giant Astra AB, for example, may have been the result of a culture that included an intensive training program that isolated recruits to indoctrinate them into the "Astra Way," an emphasis on personal attractiveness, and virtually mandatory socializing at parties with heavy drinking, dancing, and sexual indiscretions. Kimberley A. Cote, a former sales representative who settled a sexual harassment suit against the company, says, "Guys were encouraged to get as drunk as they could—and do whatever they could to the women." After numerous complaints of sexual harassment by managers at all levels of the firm, including CEO Lars Bildman, Astra's parent company suspended Bildman and launched a sweeping investigation. Bildman and other Astra USA executives deny the allegations, but the many complaints, lawsuits, and high rate of turnover among female sales reps and male managers unhappy with the firm's culture lend credence to the women's accusations. When Astra employees witnessed or heard of senior management engaging in such conduct without penalty, and observed that women who went along with the "Astra Way" received promotions while those who complained were subjected to retaliation or dismissal, how could they not get the message that sexual harassment was permissible at Astra?[7]

So many organizations fall into the trap of rewarding behavior that is inconsistent with strategic goals and workplace integrity. However, the alignment of organizational values with actual policies, evaluation systems, and other workplace systems is an integral step in achieving a high level of organizational integrity. Otherwise, employees will experience a conflict between stated goals and the behaviors necessary to achieve them. Returning to the ivy halls for an example, university professors' tenure and promotion decisions are based on a number of behaviors, including classroom teaching and research productivity. Student evaluations are usually the sole determinant of professors' success in the teaching area. These evaluations normally result in one or two composite scores (such as 4.4 on a scale of 5), which are used to rank professors within a department or college. Because teaching efficacy is normally determined from this one score, professors may be tempted to reduce course expectations and grading standards so that students will rate them more favorably. The risk with this evaluation system is that some instructors may be misled into shifting from academic standards and student learning to creating a "fun" environment. As professors Don Robin and Eric Reidenbach noted in their book, *Ethics and Profits,* "Employees will value and use as guidelines those activities for which they will be rewarded. When a behavior that is rewarded comes into conflict with an unstated and unmonitored ethical value, usually the rewarded behavior wins out."[8]

The Role of Management

Because workplace integrity involves a series of perceptions of how to act on daily issues, organizational success is determined by an employee's everyday performance in achieving company goals through legal and ethical behavior. It is up to managers and others in supervisory positions to take responsibility for the actions of their subordinates, including unethical behavior. Research suggests that successful relationships between employees and supervisors are based on openness, trust, and friendship.' These factors are very important for managers in discovering ethical issues, communicating ethical values and encouraging responsible conduct.

Top management and superiors play crucial roles in developing the culture that influences workplace integrity. Most experts agree that the chief executive officer and other managers at the executive level set the ethical tone for the entire organization. Lower-level managers take their cues from the top, yet their personal value systems also have an influence on the organization. This interplay between organizational culture and executive leadership helps determine the integrity of the firm. In addition, it is especially important to recognize that many lower and middle managers are subject to intense pressure to perform and increase profits. These pressures often involve financial goals, deadlines, competitive situations, and a lack of understanding for the reality of governmental and societal expectations. So even those employees with managerial responsibility need consistent and timely messages about the priority of workplace integrity.

The leadership style of an organization also has a great influence on employee actions. Studying the leadership styles and attitudes of an organization can help pinpoint where future ethical issues may arise. Even concerning actions that may be against the law, employees often look to their organizational leaders to determine how to resolve an issue. A recent contact lens pricing scandal at Bausch & Lomb hints at the leadership style of the company's chief executive. Both patients and optometrists took exception to Bausch & Lomb's use of three widely different pricing policies for three identical contact lens products that were differentiated only by unique brand names and usage instructions. Former CEO Daniel Gill was known as a leader who focused on financial goals, including double-digit annual growth. Some critics believe that it was Gill's insistence on such rapid growth that pushed the firm's contact lens marketing strategy into civil court over pricing issues.[10]

Leadership at every level is also important because managers can use rewards or punishments to encourage employee behavior that supports organizational goals. As we have already shown, rewards and punishment are part of the culture that influences decision making. Think about the managers you have known who balance praise for a job well done with constructive criticism for less-than-adequate performance. Although few of us really like to hear reprimands, we know that in matters of integrity, it is imperative that both positive *and* negative remarks be made. If individuals are rewarded or recognized for making the right decision, they will continue to do so; when they are punished for behaving unethically, they are unlikely to repeat the unethical behaviors.

Regardless of the organization's culture, most managers in positions of authority can exert strong pressure to ensure compliance on integrity-related issues. Alternatively, some managers avoid ethical issues and are very vague, providing almost no guidance on how to resolve ethical issues. In these cases, employees will have to interpret the organization's culture and policies on their own. This situation can become very dangerous, because a lack of leadership is likely to lead some employees to behaviors that threaten workplace integrity. And when these poor decisions become routine, it affects the organization's culture and socializes new employees into detrimental behaviors. Peer pressure is an effective force for managing ethics, including those decisions made in the workplace.

Understanding employee motivation for work success is also important in the management of others, and it helps explain many aspects of organizational integrity. For example, a person who aspires to higher positions in an organization may sabotage a coworker's project to make that person look bad. This unethical behavior is directly related to the first employee's ambition and motivation to rise in the organization. Fortunately, as people move into middle management and beyond, higher-order needs (e.g., social, esteem, and recognition) tend to become more important relative to lower-order needs (e.g., salary, safety, and job security).[11]

From a workplace integrity perspective, needs or goals may change as a person progresses through the ranks of the organization. This shift may cause or help solve problems, depending on the current ethical status of the person relative to the company or society. For example, junior executives might inflate purchase or sales orders, overbill time worked on projects, or accept cash gratuities if they are worried about providing for their families' basic needs. As they continue up the ladder and are able to fulfill these needs, such concerns may become less important. Consequently, these managers may go back to abiding by the company's policy and culture.

Examining the role of employee motivation in ethics is an attempt to relate workplace integrity with the broader social context in which workers live and the deeper moral assumptions on which society depends. Employees are individuals, and they will be motivated by a variety of personal interests. While we keep emphasizing that managers are positioned to exert pressure and obtain compliance on ethical and legal issues, we also acknowledge that an individual's personal ethics and needs will significantly affect his or her decisions.

Effective leadership in creating an ethical organizational culture is necessary for any organization to achieve an orientation of integrity. The ultimate responsibility usually rests with key executives and managers, although the leadership abilities of all employees can be utilized to create an ethical organizational culture. However, as we have repeatedly emphasized, people are only one aspect of culture. Policies and practices, both informal and formal, must be managed for ethical compliance decision making. The management of organizational integrity usually involves an analysis of situations, programs, policies, job positions, and other factors that may create pressures that challenge legal and ethical behavior.

INTERPERSONAL RELATIONSHIPS IN ORGANIZATIONS

In addition to responding to the opportunity for rewards and the leadership of managers, employees also learn about organizational integrity from the people with whom they associate in the workplace. The outcome of this learning process depends on the strength of individuals' personal values, opportunity, organizational policies, and exposure to others who behave ethically or unethically. Although persons outside the organization, such as family members and friends, also influence decision makers, we focus here on the influence of coworkers within the organization. In this section, we consider how interpersonal relationships are likely to affect the legal and ethical decisions of people in organizations.

Organizations consist of individuals and groups of people working together to achieve objectives. Getting people to work together efficiently and ethically, while coordinating the skills of diverse individuals, is a major challenge for managers. Relationships among these individuals and within groups are an important part of the proper functioning of any organization—and they play a key role in managing organizational integrity.

Individual decisions about how to react to daily problems are fundamentally influenced by observing other employees' behavior. Think for a minute about your first job. How did you learn to accomplish your goals within the organization? Who did you turn to when faced with a tough decision? Or more simply, were you more comfortable seeking guidance from your supervisor or from your close peers? These questions can help determine the informal relationships and practices (not just the formal chain of command) that employees rely on in many decision situations, including ones with implications for workplace integrity. And every organization, whether purposeful by design or as a product of its history, has a unique culture and set of practices that give employees clues about what is right and wrong on the job.

Each person in an organization has a specialized task or role in helping the organization achieve its goals. Some work on the assembly line; some do clerical work; some manage or supervise the work of others. All employees are subject to pressures and relations that may lead to ethical conflict, although these influences will vary by position, immediate work contacts, and role-specific pressures. In fact, as we discussed in the previous chapter, we have learned that it is the work group, not personal values, that potentially has the greatest effect on daily ethical decisions. In extreme situations—for instance, if asked to break into a competitor's office to obtain trade secrets—employees may abide by their own personal value systems. But in most day-to-day decisions, they tend to go along with their coworkers' wishes and beliefs on issues that appear to be defined and controlled by the work group.

It is very easy for new employees to be led into ethical conflict because they are unfamiliar with company policy or industry norms. New members of any department usually look to their peers for advice when faced with a difficult decision. Because coworkers are so important in accomplishing daily business activities, it is vital that all members support the integrity of the work group. In addition to carrying out the assigned tasks, each person is expected to act according to the role he or she occupies, not only in terms of formal job responsibilities but in terms of individual power, length of employment, and other aspects of work relations.

Consider a company that provides office supplies to a variety of businesses. Over the years the employees of this company have developed expectations as to how salespeople will carry out their assigned tasks. The current members want new recruits to accept their standards and ethical beliefs for proper behavior and therefore try to socialize them to do so. Conflict can arise when the values and norms taught through the socialization process contradict the new employee's personal values. Suppose that an experienced salesperson tells a new recruit that the company obtained an account because it gave the client the lowest estimates on some specified products. However, to make up for the lowball prices, it now provides lower-quality grades of paper and charges high rates on products for which no price had been negotiated. The new employee may find this practice deceitful and unethical. But the senior salesperson could explain that the company is providing a fair product for the price and that such a practice is common in the industry. These discussions may convince the newcomer to accept the company's views on this ethical issue.

Similar situations, in which going along with coworkers and managers may conflict with a personal standard of morality, are not uncommon in business and other types of organizations. If a person believes that his or her personal ethics severely conflict with those of the work group and of superiors, the only alternative may be to exit the organization. In the highly competitive employment market of the 1990s, quitting a job because of an ethical conflict requires a strong commitment and, possibly, the ability to survive without a job. Many people do not have the resources to go without work and obviously, in this situation, there are no easy answers to resolving such conflict.

The "grapevine" is another means by which employees can be influenced by their peers in the workplace. Although we often think of the grapevine as harmless gossip about who is or isn't in line for some promotion or who's dating whom, it can also carry informal information that reinforces the working values of the firm and shapes its culture. "Did you hear about Maria in accounting? She was fired for embezzling funds!" "You know Joe made the top salesman for the quarter again? I heard he got some of his sales by offering bribes to some customers, and that he covered his actions by fiddling with his expense reports." Such statements send messages to employees about what is expected within the company and how the company will respond. The organizational culture provides a general understanding of the behavior patterns and rules that govern an organization, but informal interactions among group members make this culture come alive and provide direction for employees' daily activities. For example, if a new employee learns through the grapevine that the organization does not punish ethical violations, he or she may seize the next opportunity for unethical behavior if it accomplishes the organization's objectives. In this case, the grapevine has clearly communicated that the organization rewards those who achieve desired objectives, even if they break rules to do so. Further, employees probably believe that the firm's managers and leaders will look the other way as long as results are obtained.

Because we have focused on how coworkers and managers have a great deal of influence on individuals' workplace integrity does not mean that these individuals are not responsible for the consequences of their behavior. Ethical decisions do not just happen in the group; obviously, they are made through human choice. Personal values do play a role in the final decision, but on work matters, group and team decisions are often used to resolve ethical and legal conflicts. In these group settings, it may be very difficult for employees even to see the consequences of their unethical or illegal decisions. And further, younger, newer, and less powerful employees may be less likely to strongly voice their opinions in these group settings.

Organizations with cultures that encourage managers and employees to act contrary to their individual ethics need to understand the costs of such conflict. Some employees succumb to organizational pressures rather than follow their own values, rationalizing their decisions by maintaining that they are simply agents of the corporation. You may have heard individuals talk about the "rules of business" as distinct from other social, personal, and cultural norms. This rationalization has several weaknesses, including the following:

▼ Organizational members can never fully abdicate their personal ethical responsibility in making decisions. Claiming to be an agent of the organization is not accepted as a legal excuse and is even less defensible from an ethical perspective.

▼ It is sometimes difficult to determine what is in the best interest of the organization. Short-term profits earned and goals reached through unethical behavior may not be in the long-run interest of the firm.

▼ Organizational members have a responsibility to parties outside the firm. Stakeholders, any group or individual who can be affected by the organization, and other concerned publics must be considered when making ethical decisions.[12]

MANAGING ORGANIZATIONAL CULTURE

In the previous chapter, we raised the idea that people who have reached the principled stages of moral development tend to act more ethically than others. This suggests that hiring people with high ethical standards can raise the ethical tone of the organization and improve daily decision making. It is also true that employees with higher expectations of punishment behave more ethically. This implies that organizational culture has a major impact on ethical decision making. A company that wants to foster ethical behavior may pursue both approaches. It may try to hire people with socially accepted ethical standards and to develop an ethical corporate culture. In other words, the system will work best if there are both good apples and good barrels. Either bad apples or bad barrels are likely to lead to ethical and legal problems. This view suggests that you *can* influence workplace integrity by nurturing organizational cultures that encourage ethical and legal behavior and discourage misconduct.

However, we have often encountered an attitude about organizational culture and workplace integrity which follows the old adage, "if it isn't broke, don't fix it." This attitude may be valid in the short run, but in today's work environment, there is no substitute for a serious analysis of how your organization is supporting integrity through its formal policies and actual practices. And as we stated in Chapter 1, integrity includes both legal and ethical responsibilities. To us, understanding and obeying the law is not enough for long-term effectiveness in the integrity area. Your organization must recognize that its culture can *and* must be managed for legal and ethical decision making, by understanding the types of signals that teach and encourage employees to make decisions that are consistent with the law and ethical standards.

Fortunately, there are a variety of policies and management tools that organizations can apply to limit the opportunity for unethical or illegal conduct. The development of codes of conduct has become a common means of attempting to manage situations that may lead to ethical or legal conflict. By communicating expectations to potential and current employees, suppliers, and others, an enforceable formal code can affect the informal culture that has developed to deal with tough situations. Essentially, management must value the role that ethics policies, coworkers, leadership style, and other organizational influences play in curbing opportunities to cross the integrity line.

The Council of Ethical Organizations has identified two areas that correlate highly with the effect of an organizational culture on ethics and legal compliance.[13] First, organizations need to examine performance and reward systems to determine whether they may inadvertently create incentives for behaviors that are contrary to ethical values and legal standards. Consider, for example, the routine use of quota systems as the overriding measure of salesperson performance. Such quota systems cannot assess the qualitative aspect of how sales are made, such as honesty and relationship building, and may unwittingly reward employees who meet sales goals with improper sales techniques. Second, organizations must focus on creating a climate where employees feel comfortable raising ethical and legal questions. In a firm where employees fear reprisal or retribution for expressing these concerns, there is little chance for creating a culture of ethical and legal compliance. A strategic focus on workplace integrity requires continuous refinement of the culture, which occurs through employee participation, top managers' willingness to support integrity initiatives, the anticipation of new risk areas, and the alignment of rewards and sanctions with the organization's ethical values and standards. In the next chapter, we expand on these ideas by discussing recent changes in the United States' legal and regulatory environment necessitating organizational cultures that value legal and ethical decision making.

Integrity Manager Checklist

The following items illustrate some of the issues that an integrity audit of your organizational culture should address. These issues can also help identify a culture that creates ethical conflict. If you answer yes to many of these questions, your organization is working to create integrity in its culture, policies, and practices. If you answer no to most of the questions, your organization needs to evaluate its focus on integrity in the workplace.

YES   NO

❏   ❏   Has the founder or top management within your firm left a legacy of integrity to the organization?

❏   ❏   Is there a shared value system and understanding of what constitutes appropriate behavior within your organization?

❏   ❏   Are there stories and myths embedded in daily conversations at work about appropriate conduct when confronting tough decisions and situations?

❏   ❏   Are there rewards for good ethical decisions even if they don't always result in a profit?

❏   ❏   Do employees in your organization have a value system of fair play and honesty toward customers?

❏   ❏   Do employees treat each other with respect, honesty, and fairness?

❏   ❏   Are there integrity-based beliefs and values about how to succeed in your organization?

❏   ❏   Are there heroes or stars in your organization that communicate a common understanding about what is important in terms of positive ethical values?

❏   ❏   Is your firm more focused long term than short run?

❏   ❏   Is your firm more externally focused on customers, the environment, and the welfare of society than internally focused in terms of its own profits?

❏   ❏   Is there open communication between superiors and subordinates to discuss ethical dilemmas?

❏   ❏   Have there been instances where employees have received advice on how to improve ethical behavior or were disciplined for committing unethical acts?

CHAPTER FIVE

INCREASING LEGAL PRESSURE FOR ETHICAL COMPLIANCE
THE FEDERAL SENTENCING GUIDELINES FOR ORGANIZATIONS

You must take on the obligation to lead this effort, to be in the forefront, not only by working to ensure that your company's employees follow the law but by embracing and placing at the very top of your company's priorities the basic good citizenship values that make law abidance possible.

> – Judge Richard P. Conaboy, Chairman, United States
> Sentencing Commission, September 7, 1995,
> speaking to "Corporate Crime in America:
> Strengthening the 'Good Citizen' Corporation"
> symposium.

In February 1996 Daiwa Bank of Japan was sentenced to pay a $340 million fine, the largest criminal fine ever assessed under U.S. law, for conspiring to conceal $1.1 billion in trading losses from federal authorities. Daiwa's top management had learned of the losses in July 1995 when a trader in the firm's New York branch confessed to superiors that he had lost $1.1 billion in concealed and unauthorized trades. The bank confirmed the wrongdoing through its own investigation in late July and early August. However, Daiwa did not disclose the losses to U.S. regulators until the end of September for several reasons. Executives wanted to wait and announce the losses along with scheduled financial reports, at which time they could write off the losses and reaffirm the bank's financial strength. They also wanted to ensure that they fully understood the extent of a very complex crime. Moreover, the Japanese Ministry of Finance had advised Daiwa executives that an immediate disclosure could have serious consequences for Japanese stock markets. While the executives' intentions were perhaps understandable, the bank's failure to report the losses promptly to U.S. federal regulators resulted in further ethical and legal issues. First, the bank falsified records to conceal the trading losses from its internal auditors. Second, U.S. government investigators later learned that Daiwa had failed to report another unauthorized trading scheme in the 1980s. Finally, prosecutors believed that the bank had misrepresented other facts to regulators in the early 1990s. Daiwa's decision to delay reporting, along with past transgressions, eventually led to the staggering fine and an eviction order from the U.S. government.[1]

Why was Daiwa fined so heavily for what essentially involved the transgressions of one employee? Beyond Daiwa's mistakes in the case, the answer lies in the Federal Sentencing Guidelines for Organizations (FSGO), enacted in 1991. These guidelines hold organizations responsible for employee misconduct. Historically, the law held accountable and punished only the individual(s) directly responsible for a violation. Under FSGO, however, the employing organization is also held accountable, responsible, and may even be indicted if a federal crime is committed by one or more employees. The sentencing guidelines also encourage companies to establish ethical and legal compliance programs. If an employee is convicted of breaking the law, under the FSGO, the sentencing court assesses the employer's efforts to prevent and detect employee misconduct. Those firms that have made sincere and effective efforts may receive abated penalties if the court believes the crime occurred despite the best efforts of the company. However, organizations that lack effective legal and ethical compliance programs may be fined and sentenced more harshly because of their failure to create ethics policies, control systems, and a culture of compliance.[2]

At Daiwa's sentencing, the company was criticized for just such a lack of internal controls and compliance efforts. Assistant U.S. Attorney Reid Figel told the court:

> [I]t is virtually impossible for any financial institution to protect itself against every potential criminal act by its employees, particularly given the highly specialized nature and complexity of the securities now traded in the world's capital markets. It is precisely because of this complexity, however, that it is essential that corporations institute and insist upon a corporate culture of absolute compliance with the rules and regulations of the marketplace. One of the most important ways to do this is to establish and enforce a system of internal controls and checks and balances that are designed to protect against the criminal acts of corporate employees.[3]

Daiwa's decision to delay reporting the unauthorized trades and the unraveling of related offenses are evidence of its failure to develop an effective compliance program. The stunning fine should serve as a forewarning for organizations that have not made a diligent and concerted effort to implement strategic integrity management.

Despite the serious ramifications associated with Federal Sentencing Guidelines for Organizations, many firms are unaware of or do not fully appreciate this change in federal regulation. If your firm does not have an effective ethical compliance program, then it is important that you recognize the risks associated with the failure to comply with this law. Because of the wide-reaching impact of this law, it is important for you to understand the FSGO, including their history, development, purpose, and impact. In this chapter, we'll describe how the FSGO apply to organizations and provide an overview of sentencing procedures and penalties. These guidelines significantly affect *all* organizations because they include incentives for firms to take steps to deter crime by establishing rigorous, effective internal compliance programs.[4] This means that if your organization is not developing and enforcing a code of conduct through training and communication, you are at risk of major penalties.

HISTORICAL BACKGROUND OF THE FEDERAL SENTENCING GUIDELINES

The Federal Sentencing Guidelines for Organizations are the result of two developments—the formation of the United States Sentencing Commission (USSC) and the Sentencing Reform Act of 1984. The USSC was created as an independent agency of the judicial branch of the federal government to establish sentencing policies and procedures for the federal justice system. A major task of the commission was to bring consistency to the decisions that courts make and to provide guidance on appropriate fines and sentences. The Sentencing Reform Act of 1984 authorized the commission to create categories of offenses (e.g., bribing governmental officials with more than $25,000) and offender characteristics (e.g., first or second offense) that are used to develop appropriate sentence and fine levels. Both the USSC and Sentencing Reform Act of 1984 were designed to enhance the ability of the federal courts to fight crime with an effective, consistent, and fair system. The USSC fulfilled part of this initiative in 1987 when it developed sentencing guidelines for individuals and antitrust sentencing for organizations. Four years later, the commission developed a detailed set of guidelines governing the sentencing of organizations, the FSGO.

One of the most significant provisos of the FSGO is that they hold organizations accountable, responsible, and even indictable for the misdeeds of their employees. In the past, most enforcement actions were limited to those employees directly responsible for an offense. The sentencing guidelines, however, hold organizations vicariously liable for all offenses committed by their agents, which is consistent with the current trend in both federal and state legislation toward organizational accountability for criminal activity. Because the FSGO have such a profound effect on organizational practices, it is useful to understand how they evolved and the philosophies that underlie them.

The Evolution of the Federal Sentencing Guidelines

The build-up to the sentencing guidelines began with both corporate crime and federal legislation.[5] In the 1960s there was extensive bid-rigging by electrical companies, and illegal payments overseas by giant government contractors were commonplace in the 1970s. The

1980s brought problems in the defense industry and pervasive insider trading and banking abuses. The Foreign Corrupt Practices Act of 1977, which, among other things, stressed the importance of developing and maintaining effective internal control systems, sent a strong signal that the government was getting serious about corporate accountability in the international marketplace. Following this act were several Security and Exchange Commission rule proposals that not only require a system for internal control but also an annual assessment of system effectiveness. Other legislation and governmental regulations that have focused on internal control mechanisms include the National Commission on Fraudulent Financial Reporting and the Federal Deposit Insurance Corporations Improvement Act of 1991. Finally, Michael Milken and Ivan Boesky also influenced the creation of the sentencing guidelines. Public outrage over their insider trading scandals influenced the Sentencing Commission's decision to link corporate criminal penalties to internal compliance programs.

Credit is also due the defense industry because its efforts in ethics and legal compliance provided much of the background for the final sentencing guideline considerations. In the 1980s, many defense contractors and related organizations began an industry effort to support corporate self-governance. The result of these efforts was the Defense Industry Initiative on Business Ethics and Conduct (DII) of 1986. Eighteen representatives from various defense contractors drafted six principles to guide the industry's efforts in business ethics and conduct (shown in Table 5-1).[6]

As the DII's efforts evolved, it established forums to discuss workplace practices and tactics that have been most effective at communicating organizational standards and linking organizational practice and policy to successful compliance. Today, the defense industry's progress in self-regulation and relations with the federal government serve as an example to organizations pursuing compliance programs in other industries.[7] The defense industry's experiences also highlight the benefits of taking a proactive stance in dealing with ethical issues and legal compliance. The industry has curbed many problem areas, improved its reputation, and developed a strong working dialogue with various agencies of the U.S. government. Despite the industry's progress, no program can completely prevent some employees from violating com-

TABLE 5-1
Principles of the Defense Industry Initiative on Business Ethics and Conduct

1. Each company will have and adhere to a written code of business ethics and conduct.

2. The company's code establishes the high values expected of its employees and the standard by which they must judge their own conduct and that of their organization; each company will train its employees concerning their personal responsibilities under the code.

3. Each company will create a free and open atmosphere that allows and encourages employees to report violations of its code to the company without fear of retribution for such reporting.

4. Each company has the obligation to self-govern by monitoring compliance with federal procurement laws and adopting procedures for voluntary disclosure of violations of federal procurement laws and corrective actions taken.

5. Each company has a responsibility to each of the other companies in the industry to live by standards of conduct that preserve the integrity of the defense industry.

6. Each company must have public accountability for its commitment to these principles.

Source: Defense Industry Initiative on Business Ethics and Conduct, 1992 Annual Report to the Public and Defense Industry, March 1993.

pany policy or the law. Therefore, when misconduct occurs, defense companies that have developed effective compliance programs should have reduced penalties.

The Philosophy Behind the Guidelines

Courts have traditionally struggled to determine appropriate ways to discipline organizations. Inconsistency plagued early sentencing decisions, and individuals were often punished for organizational strategies and managerial pressures that encouraged their misconduct. The Federal Sentencing Guidelines for Organizations were designed to hold organizations accountable for employees' illegal actions, as well as to bring consistency to the sentencing and fine structures for the resulting offenses. With this in mind, three fundamental principles guided the USSC in designing the organizational guidelines. First, the commission sought to develop a model to define the policies and actions that typify the "good citizen organization." Second, the model was designed to make organizational sentencing more fair, so that firms know what to expect when violations occur. Finally, the USSC wanted to create incentives to encourage organizations to comply with the guidelines.[8] That is, firms that persevere in developing effective compliance programs should receive less stringent penalties than those which disregard the FSGO.

At the heart of the FSGO is a "carrot-and-stick" philosophy. The "stick" is the threat of severe sanctions for organizations that do not take steps to detect and deter misconduct. Companies that strive to create effective compliance programs to forestall organizational crime may receive a "carrot" by avoiding onerous penalties should one of their employees break the law. Of course, the ultimate "stick" is organizational probation, where on-site consultants observe and monitor the organization's compliance efforts.

The USSC's underlying assumption in creating the FSGO was that organizations and the federal government could work together, not in opposition, to deter organizational crime. The guidelines therefore represent an attempt to build a quality relationship and dialogue between government and industry and within industries on the best practices and policies that discourage misconduct. This relationship has been characterized as "interactive corporate compliance," with organizations seeking more self–regulation and the government easing its control over corporate conduct.[9] Interactive compliance requires that companies actively join the fight against misconduct and that the government respond by limiting penalties for those firms that demonstrate good citizenship and a serious integrity effort.[10]

HOW THE FEDERAL SENTENCING GUIDELINES FOR ORGANIZATIONS WORK

The FSGO apply to all federal felony and Class A misdemeanor offenses committed in association with the work or activities of an organization (see Table 5-2 for examples). The guidelines apply to all types of organizations, including corporations, nonprofit entities, unions, associations, educational institutions, and governments. The city of Stilwell, Oklahoma, for example, was sued by the Justice Department for antitrust for using monopoly power over utilities customers.[11]

TABLE 5-2
Examples of Offenses Governed by the
Federal Sentencing Guidelines for Organizations

Bid–rigging (antitrust)	Extortion
Commercial bribery	Fraud
Conflict of interest	Kickbacks
Copyright and trademark infringement	Market allocation agreements (antitrust)
Eavesdropping and invasion of privacy	Payments to a public official
Embezzlement	Price–fixing (antitrust)
Evasion of export controls	Receipt of stolen property
	Transportation of hazardous materials

Source: United States Sentencing Commission, Guidelines Manual, § 3E1.1 (1994 edition).

The sentencing of organizations under FSGO is designed to accomplish four general principles:

1. The court will order the organization to remedy any harm caused by the offense.

2. If the organization operated primarily for criminal purpose, the fines will be set sufficiently high to divest the firm of all assets.

3. Fines levied against the organization are based on the seriousness of the offense and the culpability of the organization.

4. Probation is an appropriate sentence when it ensures that another sanction will be implemented or that the firm will take actions to reduce future criminal conduct.[12]

The main objectives of the FSGO are punishment, deterrence, and self–monitoring and policing. The means for achieving these objectives include mandatory restitution, monetary fines, and affirmative steps to comply with guideline incentives.[13]

Determining Fines

In the past, U.S. district judges had great discretion in imposing fines and sentences, but under the FSGO, the sentencing court applies a formula to determine the appropriate fine, which may range from $5,000 to $72,500,000. Fines assessed through the FSGO are based on the seriousness of the federal offense and the culpability or level of blame of the organization.[14] The seriousness of the offense is measured in terms of the monetary gains or losses suffered as a result of the wrongful conduct. Culpability is determined by the steps the organization has taken to prevent and detect criminal conduct. The firm's actions after the discovery of the offense and the tolerance of the offense by key personnel are also considered.

First, the sentencing court determines the base fine that can be levied against an organization committing an offense, based on the greater of either pecuniary gain (the before-tax profit gained by the organization as a result of the crime) or pecuniary loss (the monetary loss caused by the violation), or the base fine may simply be determined by the type of offense committed. The most notable exception to this rule is in the case of antitrust violations, where the base fine is relative to the volume of commerce involved.

The sentencing commission has assigned each federal crime a corresponding base offense level and a monetary value (see Table 5-3). As the offense level increases, so does the base fine that must be imposed by the sentencing court. For instance, the commercial bribery of federal, state, or local governmental officials carries a base offense level of 10. However, this level increases if the bribe exceeds $2,000. Insider trading has a base offense level of 8, with the monetary gain of the offense increasing the level by as much as 18 steps. Price–fixing and market–allocation (i.e., antitrust) agreements among competitors carry a 10 base offense level but increase as the volume of commerce exceeds $400,000. Archer-Daniels-Midland, for example, was fined a staggering $100 million after pleading guilty to price-fixing charges in 1996 because of the nature of its crime and the volume of business involved.[15]

Next, the sentencing court calculates the firm's culpability to determine the final fine. Culpability is based on three interrelated principles. First, organizations carry more blame when high–ranking individuals participate, condone, or willfully ignore criminal conduct. Second, in larger and more professional organizations, the participation, condoning, or willful ignorance of criminal conduct by high–level employees is increasingly a breach of trust and abuse of position. Third, culpability increases when there is evidence that management's tolerance of offenses is pervasive.[16]

TABLE 5-3
Base Offense Level Fines

LEVEL	AMOUNT
6 or less	$5,000
10	$20,000
15	$125,000
20	$650,000
25	$2,800,000
30	$10,500,000
35	$36,000,000
38 or more	$72,500,000

Source: United States Sentencing Commission, Guidelines Manual, § 3E1.1 (1994 edition).

The culpability score provides a minimum and maximum multiplier that courts can use to determine the fine range for an organization convicted under the FSGO. The base fine is multiplied by the applicable multipliers to determine a fine range. Tables 5-4 and 5-5 provide examples of business offenses and the steps taken to calculate the recommended fine ranges under the FSGO. These examples demonstrate how compliance programs and corporate culture can affect penalties. Remember, however, that the calculation is determined by several factors and that our examples are purely fictitious. Important factors in these cases include the size of the organization, the type of offense, the volume of commerce relative to the offense, and each firm's effort to detect, prevent, and take responsibility for the criminal conduct.

The Reality of Organizational Sentences and Fines

After doing extensive research on sentencing practices in federal courts, the USSC determined that the number of organizations sentenced each year has been fairly stable, between 300 and 400.[17] Between November 1, 1991, when the FSGO went into effect, and September 30, 1995, nearly 200 organizations were sentenced under the new guidelines.[18] Since the FSGO took effect, the Department of Justice has instructed prosecutors to apply guidelines only to offenses that occurred on or after November 1, 1991. Consequently, a number of organizations convicted through 1995 were sentenced under pre–guideline rules. In other words, current data on sentencing significantly understates the long-term implications for organizations.

TABLE 5-4
Fictitious Example of Business Offense and Fine Range

Determination: No Compliance Program

Case Facts: Acme, Inc. is a U.S.-based manufacturer of electronic component parts that employs over 5,000 individuals. The company was convicted of bribing a government official in order to secure a defense contract. The bribe was for $11 million in business contracts. Acme has no compliance program and has a reputation for tolerating and ignoring employee misconduct.

Determining fine range:

Base fine:

Base offense level	10
Contract size	15
	25 = $2.8 million base fine

Culpability score

Over 5,000 employees	+5
No compliance program	+5
	+10 = 2.0 to 4.0 multipliers
Actual fine	$5.6 million to $11.2 million

TABLE 5-5
Fictitious Example of Business Offense and Fine Range

Determination: Effective Compliance Program

Case Facts: Electro, Inc. is a manufacturer of electronic component parts that employs 1,000 individuals in the U.S. The company was convicted of price–fixing. The volume of commerce relative to the price–fixing was $700,000. The sentencing judge determined that Electro has an effective compliance program and has been diligent in its compliance and ethics efforts. Electro cooperated with the government's investigation and took ultimate responsibility for the offense.

Determining fine range:

Base fine:

20 percent of the volume of commerce	$140,000

Culpability score:

Base culpability	+ 5
Effective compliance program	- 3
Cooperate/accept responsibility	- 2
	0 = .05 to .20 multipliers
Actual fine	$7,000 to $28,000

A majority (95 percent) of the organizations sentenced under the guidelines have been closely held businesses, although more publicly traded firms are expected to be sentenced in the future. Small businesses appear to be major offenders, with most of the organizations sentenced employing fewer than 50 employees. Reasons for the relatively infrequent sentences for large, publicly traded firms include the complexity and length of the cases and prosecutors' tendency to pursue these cases in civil, rather than criminal, court.[19] These statistics are eye-opening, in that they indicate the vulnerability of small, privately-held organizations, which are less likely to have formal ethics and compliance programs modeled after the FSGO recommendations.[20] However, we know of several small companies that have established strong programs and cultures of integrity. For example, Electric Supply of Tampa, Inc., which employs fewer than 100 individuals, has developed a code of conduct, newsletter, and on-site training classes for communicating professional values, ethical standards, and compliance expectations.[21] Smaller organizations *can* create cultures of ethical compliance by implementing programs that are appropriate for their size, scope, and operations.

COMPLIANCE PROGRAM REQUIREMENTS

As we have said, the FSGO require that companies create well-planned internal ethics and compliance programs with a mandate to ensure ethical corporate cultures. An effective program must be capable of detecting and preventing crime, reducing the opportunity that employees have to engage in criminal conduct, and providing guidance for organizational decisions. Ethical and legal standards must be communicated to the entire organization, with a special focus on those departments and functions that may create greater organizational risks.[22] Codes of conduct, employee training, toll-free hot lines, newsletters, brochures, and monitoring and enforcement systems are typical components of compliance programs. The cornerstone of an effective program is "due diligence" by companies seeking to prevent and detect criminal conduct by employees.

There are general rules for establishing a program to detect and prevent criminal conduct, although the precise actions required depend on three factors. First, larger organizations must have formal, written policies defining standards and procedures for conduct. Although small organizations are also liable under the FSGO, these firms often establish ethical compliance cultures in less formal ways. However, given the number of small businesses sentenced under the FSGO, some would believe that small firms are also in need of written procedures and policies. Second, organizations must establish guidelines for specific offenses that are most likely to occur in their type of business. For instance, if a company gives salespeople great flexibility in setting prices, then it must have standards to detect and prevent price-fixing. Finally, organizations must take action to prevent offenses that have occurred in the past. The recurrence of similar offenses casts doubt on an organization's effort to prevent misconduct.

At the heart of the FSGO are seven fundamental recommendations that spell out the ideal ethical compliance policy:

1. Standards and procedures must be developed that are reasonably capable of reducing the propensity for criminal conduct.

2. Specific high-level personnel must be responsible for the compliance program.

3. Persons known to have a propensity to engage in illegal conduct must not be given substantial discretionary authority in the organization.

4. Standards and procedures must be communicated to employees, other agents, and independent contractors through training programs and publications.

5. The organization must take reasonable steps to achieve compliance with its standards, by using monitoring and auditing systems to detect criminal conduct and a reporting system that allows employees and agents to report criminal activity.

6. Standards and punishments must be enforced consistently across all employees in the organization.

7. After an offense has been detected, the organization must take all reasonable steps to respond to the offense and prevent further criminal conduct.[23]

These seven steps represent the minimum that an organization can take in demonstrating due diligence. In Chapter 6, "Developing an Effective Organizational Integrity Program," we will provide specific suggestions for creating a program that follows these seven recommendations.

But just establishing an internal compliance program is not enough. If a firm detects misconduct, then it must take appropriate disciplinary action against all individuals directly and indirectly responsible for the offense. Such sanctions should be consistent, enforceable, and appropriate for the offense. Finally, after a crime is discovered, the organization must take steps to prevent similar offenses in the future. This usually involves modifications to the compliance program, further employee training, and communications about specific types of conduct. For instance, when a top executive of a NYNEX subsidiary was indicted on insider trading charges, the company disclosed the violation in its ethics newsletter, *Ethics Leadership Review*. The company openly discussed the allegations and reminded readers of the company's policy on insider information.[24] The FSGO expects continuous improvement and refinement of ethics and compliance programs. These modifications provide more precise and effective means of detecting and preventing misconduct.

USING THE GUIDELINES FOR INTEGRITY MANAGEMENT

After years of debate over the importance of ethics in organizations, the federal government has institutionalized ethical compliance programs through the Federal Sentencing Guidelines for Organizations. While the USSC has no authority to certify organizational compliance programs, such initiatives can reduce or even eliminate penalties for organizations that are judged to have effective programs if a violation occurs. On the other hand, organizations that lack effective compliance programs may face severe maximum penalties if their employees violate the law, as Daiwa Bank of Japan learned. The FSGO indicate that the government is serious about organizational crime and will act on it accordingly. Despite this substantial change in federal law, we often encounter organizations that are unaware of the FSGO!

Some critics contend that the FSGO reward companies for doing what they are supposed to do anyway—obey the law. This criticism misses the objective of the guidelines, which is to motivate companies to develop and implement management systems to promote ethical compliance. Such systems act as buffer zones to keep employees away from legal violations. While the law attempts to deal with societal values and goals, it can set only minimal objectives. The law punishes those whom the government can prove crossed the line, and it can establish only a minimum level of ethics in society. The use of incentives allows society to apply a more open–ended standard in improving the workplace. The FSGO should inspire creativity and a greater positive effort on the part of companies than could ever be achieved by the use of threats and punishment.[25] Essentially, the guidelines encourage firms to make ethics and compliance part of the strategic management process. TECO Energy Inc. recognizes this in its Standards of Integrity manual, which is explicit about the importance of the sentencing guidelines to the company's compliance program and overall strategic direction. The manual discusses this change in federal regulation and TECO Energy's commitment to ethical business practices and strategies that ensure compliance with all laws and societal expectations.[26]

The USSC recognizes that companies are not individual citizens and do not act like individuals. While we could question the offering of rewards to individuals for simply obeying the law, it is an entirely different matter to deal with groups and organizations. Organizations generally are formed for a purpose, so offering a reward that helps a company advance toward its goals may change the way the organization acts.[27] The Defense Industry Initiative provides a good example of how a focus on ethics and compliance can create strong incentives to change the course of business practice and public accountability. The initiative is very clear on the role of company policy and culture in fostering ethical and legal decision making. Although some people believe that "good people" are sufficient to instill organizational integrity, the FSGO, DII, and examples in this chapter all point to the importance of culture, policies, and other workplace factors.

Most crimes and unethical actions are not committed by evil people bent on destroying their organizations. Instead they occur because of organizational factors, such as overly aggressive goals, reliance on financial incentives, poor communication, work group pressures, and other types of opportunity. An organization that provides incentives and opportunities for unethical activity creates a culture in which infractions are just waiting to happen. An overwhelming number of white-collar crimes stem from employee misconduct designed to benefit the organization. In such cases, employees apparently believe that organizational objectives have greater importance than legalities and ethics. An effective compliance effort should amend this belief and send a strong signal about the primacy of integrity, even in the face of stiff competition, deadlines, and other pressures. For this reason, Florida Progress Corporation's Code of Conduct makes it clear that illegal or unethical business conduct can only harm the company, and should never be construed as beneficial or appropriate.[28]

One question with which your organization may struggle is whether your compliance program is effective and represents due diligence because the guidelines are not explicit about program structure and content.[29] To meet the FSGO recommendations, your firm must create a formal process, beginning with an inventory of possible liabilities and competencies that form the foundation of your compliance program.[30] Under this process, a generic "effective" compliance program is not possible, because each organization and industry faces a unique set of legal issues and ethical dilemmas. Although you may be uncomfortable with the USSC's vagueness about an effective program, this situation is actually beneficial *and* central to the "carrot and stick" approach we discussed earlier. After all, if effectiveness were construed as having no violations, this stringent requirement would diminish the commission's inherent reward of acknowledging sincere attempts to prevent misconduct. In effect, the USSC recognizes that no compliance program can deter the determined "bad apple" employee. Instead, organizations need to understand and manage the pressures and policies that lead to ethical and ultimately legal conflict. This philosophy depicts the heart of the guideline's underlying structure—reward the organization for its ongoing attempts to apply and improve on what it has learned relative to the guidelines. Just as organizations pursue zero defects in manufacturing and other processes, they should continuously improve and refine their ethical compliance culture and related programs. In the next chapter, we provide suggestions for developing an ethics and compliance program that incorporate the FSGO recommendations.

INTEGRITY MANAGER CHECKLIST

Does your organization recognize the importance of the Federal Sentencing Guidelines for Organizations in developing policies, procedures, and an ethical compliance program? If you answer no to many of following questions, your firm needs to assess its compliance efforts. Even a number of yes responses is no guarantee of an effective compliance program as recognized by the FSGO.

YES   NO

❏   ❏   Are top managers in your organization aware of the Federal Sentencing Guidelines for Organizations?

❏   ❏   Does your organization have a code of conduct?

❏   ❏   Does your organization have an effective system for monitoring changes in federal, state, and local law?

❏   ❏   Is there an individual or department in your organization responsible for overseeing legal issues?

❏   ❏   Does your organization do background checks on new employees?

❏   ❏   Are there communications and training programs in your organization to create an effective integrity culture to prevent misconduct?

❏   ❏   Does your organization have monitoring and auditing systems to consistently enforce compliance policies?

❏   ❏   Does your organization have a method for reporting misconduct without fear?

❏   ❏   Is there a system to determine ethical and legal risks associated with your industry?

❏   ❏   Do top managers in your organization understand the ramifications of the guidelines for organizational accountability and responsibility?

❏   ❏   Is there an individual or department in your organization responsible for maintaining compliance standards and procedures?

❏   ❏   Has your organization implemented or changed company policy and programs as a result of the Federal Sentencing Guidelines for Organizations?

CHAPTER SIX

DEVELOPING AN EFFECTIVE ORGANIZATIONAL INTEGRITY PROGRAM

. . . There is, however, another more important reason why a North American 'corporate model' was not used to develop the Canadian Defence Ethics Program: the preference for values-based rather than a compliance-based ethics.

– Major Denis Beauchamp, Deputy Manager of
the Canadian Defence Ethics Program in the
Federal Ethics Report, February 1997, p. 1.

A few years ago, Orange and Rockland Utilities (O&R), based in Pearl River, NY, was rocked by scandal when several high-ranking executives were charged with embezzlement and illegal campaign contributions. The company's CEO and other senior managers were eventually dismissed. O&R tried to turn the negative experience into a positive one by applying the lessons learned to the development of a new organizational integrity initiative. The firm hired an outside Inspector General to monitor its activities and appointed a task force to develop the program. Significantly, this task force included representatives from all levels of the firm, even nonsalaried rank-and-file employees. The task force set to work developing a code of conduct and soon recommended that O&R establish an ethics office and a 12-member ethics council that includes representatives from all levels and departments of the firm, including union employees. Employees now have choices as to where to voice complaints or concerns: the Inspector General (Robert McGuire, a former New York City Police Commissioner), the ethics office (headed by Richard White, a 29-year veteran of O&R), or the ethics council. The results of O&R's integrity program have been positive. The company's new commitment to listen has even made it more amenable to input from a variety of sources, including customers, in more decision situations. Michael Donovan, O&R's Manager of Media Relations, says, "We had a good company before, but it's more integrity based now."[1]

Although there is no universally accepted approach for dealing with ethics, organizations that establish structures and cultures that foster workplace integrity are likely to encounter fewer legal and ethical crises and perhaps even improve relations with employees and customers, as O&R found. Moreover, as we indicated in the previous chapter, the Federal Sentencing Guidelines for Organizations broke new ground by codifying into law incentives for developing organizational integrity programs that promote an ethical culture and prevent employee misconduct. This chapter therefore uses the framework established by the U.S. Sentencing Commission to guide our advice for developing an organizational program for ethical compliance. This framework is consistent with current research on how to improve decision making and with the decision-making process we described in Chapter 3. Although we believe that an effective integrity program looks beyond mere legal compliance, we also believe that prudent organizations will definitely use the sentencing guidelines as a foundation for integrity initiatives.

In this chapter, we provide an overview of how you can develop an organizational integrity program, one useful for managing both legal compliance and ethical decision making. First we define an effective organizational integrity program. Then we consider the factors that are crucial for the development of such a program: codes of conduct and compliance standards; responsibility for the compliance program and the delegation of authority; effective communications and training programs; systems that monitor, audit, and enforce ethical standards in the organization; and efforts needed for continuous improvement of the compliance program.

CREATING AN EFFECTIVE ORGANIZATIONAL INTEGRITY PROGRAM

If an organization's culture and policies reward or provide opportunities to engage in misconduct through lack of managerial concern or failure to comply with the minimum requirements of the Federal Sentencing Guidelines for Organizations (see Table 6-1 for a summary of these requirements), then the organization may incur not only penalties but also the loss of customer trust, public confidence, and other intangible assets. For this reason, organizations cannot succeed solely through a legalistic approach to ethics and compliance with the sentencing guidelines; top management must cultivate high ethical standards that serve as barriers to illegal conduct. The organization must want to be a good citizen and recognize the importance of ethics to successful workplace activities and relationships.

To be a good citizen and satisfy the requirements of the FSGO, your organization should develop an *organizational integrity program* by establishing, communicating, and monitoring the ethical values and legal requirements that characterize your organization's history, culture,

TABLE 6-1
Seven Steps to Ethical Compliance

1. Develop standards and procedures to reduce the propensity for criminal conduct.

2. Designate a high-level compliance manager or ethics officer to oversee the compliance program.

3. Avoid delegating authority to people known to have a propensity to engage in misconduct.

4. Communicate standards and procedures to employees, other agents, and independent contractors through training programs and publications.

5. Establish systems to monitor and audit for misconduct and to allow employees and agents to report criminal activity.

6. Enforce standards and punishments consistently across all employees in the organization.

7. Respond immediately to misconduct and take reasonable steps to prevent further criminal conduct.

Source: United States Sentencing Commission, *Federal Sentencing Guidelines for Organizations*, 1991.

industry, and operating environment. As we have throughout the book, we use the term "integrity program" to indicate one focused on both the legal and ethical obligations of organizations.

Because it is difficult to define a generic "effective" integrity program, your organization will need to be truly reflective as you begin to develop the program's content. We recommend that you begin by analyzing the organization's current and historical ethical values. This analysis should also include a risk assessment of both internal and external issues. Usually, this information is used to create the code of conduct, which forms the foundation for the rest of the program. From here, your organization should create appropriate communication devices for delivering the integrity message. Finally, effective programs require an auditing or monitoring component to ensure continuous improvements and the correction of any deficiencies.

Creating an effective integrity program is a necessary process for ensuring that all employees understand the values of the firm and comply with policies and codes of conduct that create an ethical climate. As we have stated before, if your organization does not formally express its ethical values, then the *wrong* values may eventually become part of your culture. The Canadian military has established an ethics program that focuses on values, leadership, and the military's role in many peacekeeping obligations. The "Defence Ethics Program" is widely publicized in Canadian and other countries and is unique in its ability to balance rules and regulations with a more values-centered approach.[2] To be effective, an ethical compliance program should be communicated to all employees and others who affect workplace activities and relationships. And, just like any other organizational initiative, everyone must recognize top management's commitment to legal and ethical work practices.

One question we often hear regarding integrity programs is, "How will we know we have an effective program?" Obviously, a legal test of an ethical and legal compliance program is possible only when an individual employee or the employing organization is charged with a crime. In the process of an investigation, the court system evaluates organizational responsibility for the individual's behavior. If the organization contributed to the wrongdoing or failed to exercise due diligence in preventing the crime, then both the individual *and* the organization may be punished under the FSGO. The presence of an effective organizational integrity program should help reduce the possibility of penalties and negative public reaction should a violation occur. However, a program developed in the absence of misconduct will be much more effective than one imposed as a reaction to misconduct. The ethical test of an integrity program can be evaluated on the day-to-day decisions by employees as it relates to industry standards, community standards, or the acceptance of the firm's conduct by important publics, including customers and other partners.

ESTABLISHING CODES OF ETHICS AND COMPLIANCE STANDARDS

The best place to begin when creating an organizational integrity program is to establish organizational standards of conduct. These standards may take the form of codes of conduct or policy statements. Employees who come from different cultures and backgrounds and have different moral philosophies are likely to have difficulty determining what behavior is acceptable in the workplace without uniform policies and standards. Codes of conduct—formal statements of what an organization expects in the way of ethical behavior—let employees know what behaviors are acceptable or improper.

If you are developing a code of conduct from scratch, you may want to start by looking at other companies' codes, especially those of other firms within your industry. However, your code of ethics should reflect your firm's needs, issues, practices, and history, so other codes should serve only as guides for your own effort. Our Web site, as listed in the Preface, includes hotlinks to the codes of ethics of many organizations that may provide some ideas for your own code.

After reviewing dozens of codes of conduct, we have developed a number of guidelines to help you draft an effective document.

1. **Upper-level management should provide leadership.** The inescapable truth is that those who are in leadership positions determine the moral and ethical tone of an organization. A code of ethics should reflect senior management's desire for organizational compliance with the values, rules, and policies that support an ethical

and legal climate. Development of a code of ethics should definitely involve the firm's highest officers, including the president, board of directors, and senior managers who will be implementing the code. However, we also believe that codes of conduct should be developed with input from employees at all levels. Otherwise, your organization runs the risk of writing an incomplete policy and/or failing to create widespread "buy in" for the standards. Legal staff should be called upon to ensure that the code has correctly assessed key areas of risk and that potential legal problems are buffered by standards in the code.

2. **Identify the principle uses, purposes, and stakeholders of the code.** The CEO and upper management must next identify the firm's key objectives which will later serve as the ground rules in the code. As a result, top management must make their expectations explicit. In this way they can guide the firm in identifying other ethical business objectives.

3. **Define essential values.** Your code should explain the underlying organizational values and principles that support it. Levi Strauss & Co., for example, has defined six values—honesty, promise-keeping, fairness, respect for others, compassion, and integrity—that guide everything the firm strives to do.³ These values should define the culture and set the overall tone for organizational decisions. Such values may sometimes sound esoteric (e.g., "Our company believes in being honest and true."), but they are usually derived from the organization's vision or mission statements and are important for guiding and implementing specific behaviors. These values must be explained in the code—with plenty of examples of how employees can carry them out.

4. **Differentiate between ethical and legal standards of conduct.** The code should educate employees so that they understand that ethics and the law follow a continuum and that the law is predicated upon the standards and expectations of society and not vice versa. Making this distinction will give employees a better understanding of why it is important to make ethical standards the norm in order to buffer legal issues. It may be prudent for your code to discuss spe-

cific statutes and regulations that affect your firm and industry. For example, British Gas' documents explain that it is a criminal offense to accept or solicit gifts as an inducement or reward. Your firm should also explain why "ethical" behavior that exceeds the minimum legal requirement is important and necessary to the organization's success.

5. **Make the ethics code relevant, credible, and concise.** Codes of ethics cannot solve every ethical dilemma, but they should provide rules and guidance for employees to follow. Your code should address the most common concerns your firm faces in a variety of situations, from internal operations to financial disclosure practices, and relate them to actual organizational policies. The code should be specific enough to be reasonably capable of preventing misconduct. Codes that communicate very generally, at the level of "do no harm" or "be fair and honest," are not enough; they must provide sufficient direction for employees to avoid risks associated with their particular businesses. Codes that do not confront specific high-risk activities within the scope of daily operations are inadequate for maintaining standards that can prevent misconduct. For example, in the retail food industry, food-stamp fraud totals over $1 billion a year, and is especially problematic among small firms. With state and federal governments stepping up investigations of food-stamp fraud, the redemption of food stamps should be a high-risk issue for retail food chains.[*] A code of ethics for such retailers could address the need to maintain strict compliance with food-stamp redemption policies.

    If your firm does business outside your own country, your code should also address legal and ethical issues that may arise in international business. The code should also be specific in addressing its constituencies. Typically codes address the interests of customers, other consumers, suppliers, governments, competitors, local communities, shareholders and even employee families. Your ethics objectives should be consistent with organizational functions. The code should also be operationally relevant with specific examples so that it can be used in employees' everyday decision making. This can be accomplished by linking the code to employee policy manuals, the firm's internal planning process, evaluation systems, marketing plans, and other formal documents. Also, to assure adequate coverage of the major concerns, the code should contain multiple topical sections, perhaps organized into the categories we suggested in Chapter 2.

6. **Include formal mechanisms for resolving ethical issues.** Your code of conduct should serve as a resource guide—one that employees will refer to for answers to difficult situations. For this reason, we recommend that the code include a description of departments and employees that handle or help resolve legal and ethical dilemmas. The description of 1-800 hot lines as well as designated ethics officers within the code helps to cement the code into place and further prove to the organizational culture the importance of such standards and values.

7. **Have a small representative group write the draft.** In choosing a small group to actually draft the code, you should make sure that they represent the company's departments and power groups. Such a group could include representatives from human resources, finance, marketing, general management, and the board of directors. You should also include input from a wide variety of groups such as focus groups, top executives, management personnel, and employees. This collaborative approach should decrease the likelihood that a particular group feels neglected or ostracized, which helps when the code must be enforced or changed. Moreover, these groups may bring unique perspectives and ideas to the process. O&R's ethics task force, which included members from all levels of the organization, brought practical suggestions to the process that ultimately helped implement the ethics program more effectively. For example, one member of the task force, a surveyor who spent much of his work day in the field, suggested distributing the code in a small, handbook-size booklet rather than a big binder so that employees could easily carry the booklet in their trucks. He felt a big binder would probably stay in employees' lockers, unused.[5] The use of outside focus groups may identify issues that might be important to consumers or channel members but unimportant within the firm or industry before they become legal concerns. Finally, if you have

foreign subsidiaries, you may want to create codes in different languages and with respect for different country-specific laws and customers. Honeywell, for example, has translated its code of ethics into six languages and has several communications tools that address ethical and legal issues in a variety of countries.[6]

8. **Have upper management and a sample group of employees, channel members, and customers review the code.** After a small group has drafted the initial code, it is helpful to have a larger group review it and to create a feedback loop. If only a small group reviews the document, it may be devoid of key ethical areas. Because of some companies' myopic focus on the bottom line, many issues such as the environment, the social welfare of the community, or employee rights can be missed. The review of the document by different groups brings different perspectives to the issues addressed in the code. Further, the review process begins the process of "buy in" and continuous improvement for the total integrity effort. In addition, this group should look for a writing style that balances prohibitive ("thou shalt not") with a more affirmative tone that focuses on the positive aspects on integrity in the workplace.

9. **Have all employees read and sign the code with periodic revisions.** By distributing the final document to every employee and having them review and sign it, you make the code a physical entity within their lives. Many good managers create a reminder for employees by periodically reviewing various aspects of the code, perhaps on how it relates to an emerging issue in the news. This reinforces the importance of the document instead of merely having employees sign it once a year. Also, requesting written comments about provisions that work or don't work will help you in the revision process as well as identify ethical areas of concern.

APPOINTING A HIGH-LEVEL MANAGER TO OVERSEE THE COMPLIANCE PROGRAM

An integrity program will be significantly enhanced by making a high-level manager or a committee responsible for its administration and oversight. The executive in charge of the compliance program is typically called the ethics officer, compliance officer, or compliance coordinator. In large corporations, one or more senior managers are usually appointed to serve as compliance or ethics officers, but the entire senior management should support and be involved in the ethical compliance process. Sometimes, a special committee of senior managers, other employees, and/or the board of directors will also oversee the company's ethical compliance program.[7] Remember that O&R has both an ethics officer and an ethics council, with the latter composed of representatives from throughout the firm. In smaller organizations, the ethics officer may be the owner, executive director, or other top manager of the firm. Even in those organizations with few formal titles, someone should have primary responsibility for ensuring a focus on workplace integrity. We know that some smaller firms may not see a need for such a formal approach to workplace integrity. However, the fact is that under the sentencing guidelines, a clear majority of the prosecuted cases involve small businesses. Moreover, small organizations are more likely to be victims of employee fraud than large businesses.[8]

Ethics officers, or those individuals with oversight for ethical compliance, usually have the following responsibilities:

- ▼ Coordinating the integrity program with top management, and, if applicable, the board of directors
- ▼ Developing, revising, and disseminating a code of conduct
- ▼ Developing effective communication and training devices
- ▼ Establishing audit and control systems to determine the effectiveness of the program
- ▼ Reviewing and modifying the integrity program to improve its effectiveness
- ▼ Monitoring changes in the industry and environment that may affect organizational integrity
- ▼ Dealing with internal issues, including employee questions, concerns, and complaints

Regardless of how the oversight of the integrity program is handled, it is important that the managers in charge of the integrity initiative tailor it to the scope, size, and history of the organization. Just as important is reviewing the need for special compliance components based on the organization's legal history, industry standards, and regulatory concerns. High risk areas should be given special attention and preventive measures integrated into the program. Furthermore, without an effective manager in charge of the ethics program, it will be impossible to develop organizational learning and records that document the company's steps in managing the program.

Although it may seem obvious, it is important that the ethics officer or manager who oversees the integrity program avoid delegating substantial discretionary authority to people who are known to engage in misconduct. Information in the personnel files, the results of company audits, managers' opinions, and other available information should be used to ascertain the likelihood that managers will engage in misconduct. An adequate investigation should also be conducted before hiring individuals who have been convicted of offenses, if the firm knows—or should know—about these convictions. This is not to say that such people should not be hired; however, when past wrongdoing is uncovered—for instance, if the individual in question has been convicted of a felony or fired for misconduct in another organization— then the firm should exercise care in delegating authority to that person. Those in charge of ethical oversight within the organization have the obligation to prevent unethical people from holding positions of authority.

COMMUNICATING STANDARDS

Managers cannot motivate employees or coordinate their efforts without proper communication. It is especially important to help employees identify ethical and legal issues and give them the means to address and resolve such issues in ambiguous situations. Organizations can communicate their integrity standards and other ethical compliance messages through training, publishing the code of ethics, having employees sign the code of ethics, and creating various reminders throughout the year. Northern Telecom (Nortel), a Toronto-based telecommunications firm, even posts its code of conduct on its World Wide Web site on the Internet so that suppliers, shareholders, and prospective employees can easily view the firm's standards and policies. In addition, employees need guidance on where to go for assistance from managers or other designated personnel in resolving ethical problems.

Communication by top executives keeps the firm on its ethical course, and these executives must ensure that the ethical climate is consistent with the company's overall objectives. Communication is important in providing guidance for ethical standards and activities that provide integration between the functional areas of the business. A vice president of marketing, for example, must communicate and work with regional sales managers and other marketing employees to ensure that all agree on what constitutes certain unethical activities, such as bribery, price collusion, and deceptive sales techniques. No program can be implemented without complete understanding of its objectives and employee cooperation to make it work. While most managers and employees don't have "ethics" in their job title, under the FSGO, everyone is accountable.

To communicate ethical values and implement an effective integrity program, training is necessary. Ethics and legal compliance programs need to educate employees about formal ethical frameworks and models for analyzing ethics issues. Employees can then base their decisions on policy, accepted practice, and knowledge of choices, rather than on pure emotions and pressures felt in the thick of tough situations. In Chapter 7, we provide specific guidance on developing an effective integrity communications and training initiative.

IMPLEMENTING THE INTEGRITY PROGRAM: ENFORCING, MONITORING, AND AUDITING STANDARDS

Implementing a program that encourages employees to make more ethical and legal decisions is not very different from implementing other types of organizational strategies. Implementation in workplace integrity requires designing activities to achieve organizational objectives ethically and legally, using available resources and given existing constraints. Implementation translates a plan for action into operational terms and establishes a means by which organizational integrity will be enforced, monitored, and audited.

A firm's ability to plan and implement integrity standards depends in part on how it structures resources and activities to achieve its objectives. For example, ever since its founding in 1850, apparel manufacturer Levi Strauss & Co. has communicated company values—what it stands for and what its people believe in, as well as its tradition of always treating people fairly and caring about their welfare.[10] The firm's mission and aspirations statements (see Table 6-2) tell how the business should be run. People's attitudes and behavior must be guided by a shared commitment to the business instead of by obedience to traditional managerial authority. Encouraging diversity of perspectives, disagreement, and the empowerment of people helps align the company's leadership with its employees.

Enforcing Integrity Standards

Consistent enforcement and necessary disciplinary action are essential to an effective integrity program. When employees comply with organizational standards, their efforts should be acknowledged and rewarded, perhaps through public recognition, bonuses, raises, or some other means. Conversely, when employees deviate from organizational standards, they should be reprimanded, transferred, docked, suspended, or even fired. The ethics or compliance officer is usually responsible for implementing all disciplinary actions the organization takes for violations of its ethical standards. Many companies are including ethical compliance in employee performance appraisals. During performance appraisals, employees may be asked to sign an acknowledgement that they have read the current guidelines on workplace ethical policies. In addition, an integrity-focused supervisor should also discuss the workplace pressures that can create ethical conflict.

Monitoring and Auditing Ethical Compliance

Monitoring compliance is an ongoing activity that usually involves comparing employee performance with the organization's integrity standards. Ethical compliance can be measured through the observation of employees and a proactive approach to dealing with ethical and legal issues. An effective ethical compliance program uses both investigatory and reporting resources, such as a "help line." Sometimes external auditing and review of other organizations' activities is helpful in developing benchmarks of compliance.

To determine whether a person is performing his or her job ad-

TABLE 6-2
Levi Strauss's Statement of Mission and Aspirations

Levi Strauss & Co. Mission Statement

The mission of Levi Strauss & Co. is to sustain profitable and responsible commercial success by marketing jeans and selected casual apparel under the Levi's brand.

We must balance goals of superior profitability and return on investment, leadership market positions, and superior products and service. We will conduct our business ethically and demonstrate leadership in satisfying our responsibilities to our communities and to society. Our work environment will be safe and productive and characterized by fair treatment, teamwork, open communications, personal accountability and opportunities for growth and development.

Aspiration Statement

We all want a Company that our people are proud of and committed to, where all employees have an opportunity to contribute, learn, grow, and advance based on merit, not politics or background. We want our people to feel respected, treated fairly, listened to and involved. Above all, we want satisfaction from accomplishments and friendships, balanced personal and professional lives, and to have fun in our endeavors.

When we describe the kind of LS&CO we want in the future what we are talking about is building on the foundation we have inherited: affirming the best of our Company's traditions, closing gaps that may exist between principles and practices and updating some of our values to reflect contemporary circumstances.

What Type of Leadership Is Necessary to Make Our Aspirations a Reality

New Behaviors: Leadership that exemplifies directness, openness to influence, commitment to the success of others, willingness to acknowledge our own contributions to problems, personal accountability, teamwork and trust. Not only must we model these behaviors but we must coach others to adopt them.

Diversity: Leadership that values a diverse workforce (age, sex, ethnic group, etc.) at all levels of the organization, diversity in experience, and a diversity in perspectives. We have committed to taking full advantage of the rich backgrounds and abilities of all our people and to promote a greater diversity in positions of influence. Differing points of view will be sought; diversity will be valued and honesty rewarded, not suppressed.

Recognition: Leadership that provides greater recognition—both financial and psychic—for individuals and teams that contribute to our success. Recognition must be given to all who contribute: those who create and innovate and also those who continually support the day-to-day business requirements.

Ethical Management Practices: Leadership that epitomizes the stated standards of ethical behavior. We must provide clarity about our expectations and must enforce these standards through the corporation.

Communications: Leadership that is clear about Company, unit, and individual goals and performance. People must know what is expected of them and receive timely, honest feedback on their performance and career aspirations.

Empowerment: Leadership that increases the authority and responsibility of those closest to our products and customers. By actively pushing responsibility, trust and recognition into the organization we can harness and release the capabilities of all our people.

Source: Levi Strauss & Co. Reprinted by permission.

equately and ethically, observation might focus on how the employee handles an ethically charged situation. For example, many businesses use role playing in the training of salespeople and managers. Ethical issues can be introduced into the discussion, and the results can be videotaped so that both the participants and the superior can evaluate the results of the ethical dilemma.

Questionnaires that survey employees' perceptions of the ethics of their superiors, coworkers, and themselves, as well as ratings of ethical or unethical practices within the firm and industry, can serve as benchmarks in an ongoing assessment of ethical performance. Then, if unethical behavior is perceived to increase, management will have a better understanding of what types of misconduct are occurring and why. A change in the ethics training within the company may be necessary.

The existence of an internal system for employees to report wrongdoing is especially useful in monitoring and evaluating ethical performance. A number of firms have set up ethics hot lines to offer support and give employees an opportunity to register ethical concerns. While there is always some worry that people may misreport a situation or misuse the hot line to retaliate against another employee, hot lines have become widespread and employees do utilize them. When NYNEX Corporation set up an ethics hot line, for example, it received over 2,700 calls in one year; however, only 10 percent of the calls dealt will alleged misconduct.[11]

Effective monitoring systems also require prompt investigation of any known or suspected misconduct. The ethics officer or other appropriate employee needs to make a recommendation to senior management on how to deal with a particular ethical infraction. In some cases, a company may be required to report substantiated misconduct to a designated governmental or regulatory agent in order to receive credit under the Federal Sentencing Guidelines for Organizations for having an effective compliance program.[12]

An ethical compliance audit is a systematic and objective evaluation of an organization's ethics program and/or performance to determine its effectiveness. In particular, it is useful to focus on the key factors that influence how ethical decisions are made, including organizational culture, peers, superiors, and formal systems of reward and punishment. Understanding the ethical issues in an audit can help in refining codes of ethics and developing other programs to encourage ethical behavior in your organization.

The ethical compliance audit in Table 6-3 and the Integrity Manager Checklists at the end of each chapter in this book offer examples of items that could be used to assess an organization's ethical concerns and control mechanisms. The specific issues given in Table 6-3 to monitor in an ethics audit are given as examples, and the questions contain judgments of behavior. Like an accounting audit, an ethics audit may be more helpful if someone with expertise from outside the organization conducts the audit. However, we recommend that your organization participate in the development of the audit tool to ensure that the

TABLE 6-3
Examples of Issues That Could Be Monitored in an Ethics Audit

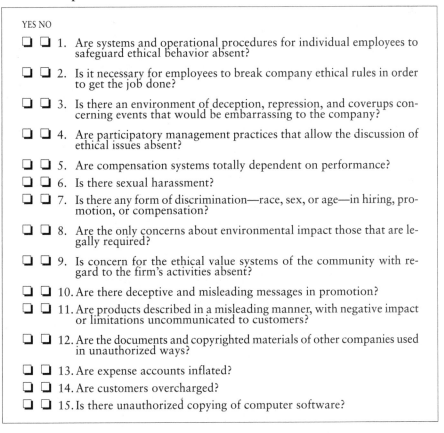

YES NO

1. Are systems and operational procedures for individual employees to safeguard ethical behavior absent?

2. Is it necessary for employees to break company ethical rules in order to get the job done?

3. Is there an environment of deception, repression, and coverups concerning events that would be embarrassing to the company?

4. Are participatory management practices that allow the discussion of ethical issues absent?

5. Are compensation systems totally dependent on performance?

6. Is there sexual harassment?

7. Is there any form of discrimination—race, sex, or age—in hiring, promotion, or compensation?

8. Are the only concerns about environmental impact those that are legally required?

9. Is concern for the ethical value systems of the community with regard to the firm's activities absent?

10. Are there deceptive and misleading messages in promotion?

11. Are products described in a misleading manner, with negative impact or limitations uncommunicated to customers?

12. Are the documents and copyrighted materials of other companies used in unauthorized ways?

13. Are expense accounts inflated?

14. Are customers overcharged?

15. Is there unauthorized copying of computer software?

key issues your employees confront are included. Top management should get involved in determining the specific legal and ethical issues to evaluate, based on the company's desired integrity perspective. Where concerns are found, the audit can help management refine or establish ethics policies as guidelines for employee actions.

CONTINUOUSLY IMPROVING
THE ETHICAL COMPLIANCE PROGRAM

To promote ethical and legal behavior, your firm's policies, rules, and standards must be assimilated into its compliance system. Reducing unethical or illegal behavior is a goal no different from reducing costs, increasing profits, or improving quality. An integrity program that is aggressively enforced and integrated into the corporate culture can be effective in improving ethical and legal behavior within the organization.

If the auditing process, or worse, a major legal infraction, indicates that the integrity program has not been effective at deterring misconduct, the program should be modified as necessary. After a Kmart executive was indicted for accepting kickbacks, for example, the retail giant recognized a need to revise and expand its code of ethics to be more specific. The firm's new code explicitly directs employees not to take bribes, kickbacks, loans, gratuities, and other solicitations from suppliers. It also includes a vow to turn in any employee or business associate who violates the code. Even more significantly, Kmart now requires vendors, as well as employees, to sign annual statements pledging they will abide by the code.[13] Organizations may also need to consider setting higher standards, improving reporting processes, making punishments more severe, improving communication of standards and training programs, as well as participating in above-board discussions with other organizations. Most ethics officers we know are very willing to share their "best practices" and ideas for improvement.

If an organization determines that its performance has not been satisfactory in ethical terms, management may want to reorganize the way certain kinds of decisions are made. For example, a decentralized organization may need to centralize key decisions, if only for a time, so that top-level managers can ensure that the decisions are ethical.

Centralization may reduce the opportunity for lower-level managers and employees to make unethical decisions. Top management can then focus on improving the corporate culture and infusing more ethical values throughout the organization by providing rewards for positive behavior and sanctions for negative behavior. In other firms, decentralization of important decisions may be a better way to attack ethical problems, so that lower-level managers, familiar with the forces of the local business environment and local culture and values, can make more decisions. Whether the ethics function is centralized or decentralized, the key need is to delegate authority in such a way that the organization can achieve its standards for workplace integrity.

Although we can provide general advice for creating an effective organizational integrity program, it is really up to top management and other employees to determine what is right for your organization. There is a growing number of consultants who specialize in the ethics and legal compliance area who can assist your firm with creating a strong integrity effort. However, we emphasize that a generic program is not enough to satisfy either the sentencing guidelines or this book's philosophy of workplace integrity. Ultimately, your organization must make the commitment to evaluate its risks, culture, employees, and constituents and then go through the long process of internalizing an ethical culture and operating environment. There will be some setbacks and it is a multi-year proposition, with the need to continuously refine and improve.

The Federal Sentencing Guidelines for Organizations provide a generic framework for developing an ethical compliance program. The seven steps, as we have discussed, should serve as the starting point for implementing an integrity program that is effective for your particular risk areas, organizational culture, employees, industry, and strategic orientation. We do *not* believe that the seven steps are the only solution for managing workplace integrity. Rather, they are important at a very basic level—your organization needs to respond to changing expectations for legal compliance and to succinctly communicate its integrity effort. In other words, if you honestly and conscientiously use these seven steps, you should at least have an ethical compliance framework that customers, suppliers, government, and other members of society can easily recognize and understand. However, we expect that most organizations will elect to go beyond the sentencing guidelines— and create a powerful organizational culture that goes above the law in its integrity expectations.

INTEGRITY MANAGER CHECKLIST

The following questions can assist your organization in understanding the types of issues that contribute to the development of an effective ethical compliance program. A high number of yes answers indicate that ethical control mechanisms and procedures are in place in your organization. Statements to which you answer no will require specific attention in your ongoing ethical compliance efforts.

YES   NO

❏   ❏   Is your organization's integrity effort the result of input from many departments and levels of authority?

❏   ❏   Are there mechanisms in place to avoid delegating authority to individuals with a propensity for misconduct?

❏   ❏   Does your organization communicate its integrity standards to suppliers, customers, and others that have a relationship with the organization?

❏   ❏   Do organizational manuals and written documents guiding operations contain messages about ethical and otherwise appropriate behavior?

❏   ❏   Is there formal communication within your organization about procedures and activities that are considered acceptable ethical behavior?

❏   ❏   Does top management have a mechanism to detect ethical issues relating to employees, customers, the community, and society?

❏   ❏   Is there consistent enforcement of standards and punishments across the organization?

❏   ❏   Is there an ethics committee, department, team, or group that deals with ethical issues in your organization?

❏   ❏   Is there a concerted attempt at continuously improving the ethical compliance program within your organization?

CHAPTER SEVEN

IMPLEMENTING ETHICS AND LEGAL COMPLIANCE TRAINING

We have to start, then, toward understanding how to make corporate values work. They have to be compatible with the culture that's already there; pretty words won't bloom in the wrong soil. Values are living things. You can't just stick them in a vase and leave them. You have to manage them. Work with them. Keep them alive.

– Thomas A. Stewart, writing in *Fortune*
magazine, June 10, 1996.

Tenet Healthcare Corporation, one of the largest hospital operators in the United States, is focused on creating an integrity program that sets the standard for all health care companies seeking effective ethical and legal compliance. At Tenet, ethics and compliance are part of a holistic approach to workplace integrity. All of Tenet's 105,000 employees and its board of directors undergo compliance training, starting with a brief orientation to Tenet's corporate philosophy on integrity within four weeks of employment. After this, employees receive two hours of training that focuses on the company's code of conduct. Tenet also requires employees to attend annual refresher courses that reinforce its basic values of quality, honesty, reliability, and good corporate citizenship. Tenet has about 100 in-house facilitators from various hospitals who volunteer their time and talent to corporate integrity training. However, these volunteers do not conduct training in their own hospitals; instead, they travel to other Tenet facilities, delivering over 200 training sessions a year. Because employees perceive these trainers as being "from outside," they may feel more comfortable raising issues that occur in their own hospitals. Because of the trainers' intimate knowledge of the industry and corporate culture, employees can also be confident that the trainer's message is well informed, based on the firm's standard of conduct, and free of personal issues that may inhibit working relationships between management and other employees. Although Tenet's Corporate Integrity Program was born as a result of a number of legal and ethical issues that Tenet faced in the early 1990s, the company has now moved to a level of commitment in its integrity effort that should be of interest to many readers.[1]

Tenet's commitment to organizational integrity has nurtured the success of its ethical compliance program. However, many critics of integrity efforts have expressed valid concerns that such programs are often just "window dressing," merely public relations tools or mechanisms to protect the company in case of legal problems. When an organization fails to properly implement an integrity initiative, the program will be of limited value, even in legal disputes. In fact, the Council of Ethical Organizations has found that employees believe that legalistic codes of conduct are generally ineffective at influencing behavior; moreover, they often assume such codes were developed to protect the company, not to promote organizational integrity.[2] In such cases, the ethical compliance policy truly does become window dressing, just another document hanging on the wall in an office reception area. Or perhaps employees acknowledge it only when they certify annually that they have read the code of conduct. Such a policy has no real meaning to employees on a daily basis, and it contributes little to an effective compliance program that fosters corporate integrity and satisfies the requirements of the Federal Sentencing Guidelines for Organizations.

It is only through creative, well-planned training and implementation strategies, like those employed by Tenet, that organizations can avoid the pitfalls of "window dressing" and "policy without implementation." In this chapter, we therefore focus on implementing an organizational integrity program that follows the recommendations of the U.S. Sentencing Commission *and* reflects your organization's unique circumstances. In particular, we will discuss the role of training in an overall ethical compliance effort, introduce a variety of training and educational tools, and provide examples from organizations.

THE IMPORTANCE OF
ETHICS AND COMPLIANCE TRAINING

In Chapters 5 and 6, we discussed seven steps that the FSGO recommend organizations take in exercising due diligence and developing an effective organizational integrity program. Of these steps, the fourth and seventh are especially relevant for understanding the importance of training and education efforts.

Step four states that, "Standards and procedures must be communicated to employees, other agents, and independent contractors through training programs and publications." This statement emphasizes the importance of implementation and organizations' obligation to educate employees about ethics and legal compliance. Companies that have effective programs understand their employee base, major risk areas, culture, industry, and other factors that influence training design. Consequently, these organizations have committed the necessary resources to create training programs and ongoing communications systems that reflect their internal and external environments. Small businesses and nonprofit organizations can also apply the logic of internal analysis and environmental scanning to determine their educational needs in implementing effective ethical compliance programs.

Step seven, which says, "After an offense has been detected, the organization must take all reasonable steps to respond to the offense and prevent further criminal conduct," stresses that companies need to continuously refine and communicate their organizational integrity expectations. This implies a need to evaluate and improve the compliance program based on feedback. Obviously, a legal infraction will cause much turmoil and may indicate that changes are needed in policy and implementation strategy. For example, after Northrop Corporation (now Northrop Grumman) experienced a number of civil and criminal lawsuits as a result of aggressive business practices, it initiated comprehensive ethics and compliance improvements. A training program was developed that effectively communicated company expectations for ethical compliance. Today, Northrop is recognized for its cutting-edge approach to strategic integrity management.[3]

The aftermath of a Treasury bond-bidding scandal at Salomon Brothers also demonstrates the importance of swift action under the FSGO. Shortly after the scandal came to light, Warren Buffett, the firm's biggest shareholder and a man with a reputation for integrity, was installed as interim chairman of Salomon. Within a month, Buffett severed all ties with the top managers responsible for the legal infraction, sent a letter of apology to all employees and their families, and began to implement improved ethics and compliance systems.[4] Step seven of the FSGO requirements is explicit about the actions needed after a criminal offense has occurred. However, organizations with strong compliance efforts often detect problems before they become legal issues.

Although the sentencing guidelines are explicit about the role of training and education in an effective compliance effort, many firms already implement training as an integral part of employee and organizational development. If training is viewed only as a means of seeking due diligence, then it is easy to fall into the trap of emphasizing legal compliance at the expense of organizational integrity. As you will see in Chapter 10, some large corporations, including Texas Instruments and Lockheed Martin, have developed separate workshops and seminars for compliance, ethics, and substantive business practices. Not all organizations have the resources, or perhaps the need, to create such specialized workshops. If your organization is dedicated to integrity management, then training and education should be used to reinforce the core values, cultural elements, and policies that buffer misconduct. In fact, there is little chance of creating a high integrity workplace without training, educating, and reinforcing ethical values. Although the law forms the basis for many decisions, research suggests that an overly legalistic approach to workplace integrity is rarely appreciated, taken seriously, or trusted by employees. Your organization must create a solid connection between its mission, ethical values, and culture and the policies and systems designed to prevent legal violations.

DESIGNING A TRAINING PROGRAM

An implicit goal of organizational integrity programs should be to give employees and other agents the capacity to make ethical and legal decisions. Reaching this goal requires several training design elements. First, employees need to be educated about company policy and expectations, laws and regulations, and general societal standards. Second, employees need to be made aware of available resources, support systems in place, and designated personnel with responsibility for managing the integrity effort. Third, employees need to feel empowered to make the "right" decision and to ask tough questions. This requires an organizational culture and management style that invite serious discussion about ethical dilemmas. Finally, training and communication efforts need to be linked with all aspects of organizational integrity. For example, if your ethics officer is fielding questions about a particular company practice, then he or she should focus on that issue in upcoming communications and training sessions. Many organizations routinely use their publications to reinforce and clarify standards. USF&G's company newsletter regularly features a section highlighting a legal or ethical question that is relevant to its employees. The question is followed by a detailed response written by a senior manager, using company policy and the law as rationale. Even small steps such as this go a long way in keeping ethics and compliance a strategic and tactical priority.

Training and communication efforts for ethical and compliance issues should reflect each firm's unique characteristics, including its history, culture, size, management style, employee base, and core values. Integrity training programs should also take into account those issues that face many organizations, such as industry norms, laws and regulations, and general societal expectations. To accomplish this, the Florida Progress Corporation has incorporated three basic training elements into its compliance program. First, all employees are educated about the company's ethics and legal compliance initiatives. Second, supervisors and employees are trained in their specific duties and responsibilities under the program. Finally, employees are routinely informed of new information on compliance issues and changing expectations. However, there is no single model for dealing with ethical compliance and developing an effective training and education program. Even the writers of the sentencing guidelines recognized that different organizations will use different techniques to communicate ethical and legal expectations.

Successful reporting systems, such as confidential hot lines and help lines, should provide data on the types of ethical and legal issues that are causing concern within the organization. Lockheed Martin, for example, maintains a 24-hour employee hot line. The company wants employees to be able to express their concerns to a company representative, even if it's 2:00 in the morning. The data obtained from such reporting systems should be analyzed and converted into information that is used to improve a strategic integrity focus. When assessing employee complaints, Lockheed Martin noticed that they now focus less on legal and compliance issues and instead show greater concern for human resources policies and decisions, information that the firm can use to modify these policies or communicate them in a different manner. The Center for Business Ethics at Bentley College has found that over 60 percent of all help line calls focus on human resources issues, such as job promotions and raises. This finding may be the result of a "disconnection" between organizations' and employees' priorities, where employees perceive ethical compliance in terms of fairness and personnel, not in the broader context of legal compliance, social responsibility, and strategic integrity. Such information may suggest changes in how an organization communicates and implements its ethical compliance program.

In addition to understanding organizational and industry factors, creating an effective training program for ethical compliance requires an understanding of a variety of disciplines, including adult education, organizational behavior, psychology, and sociology. Although ethics officers, top executives, and managers may not be students of these disciplines, they do have oversight and responsibility for implementing ethics and compliance training.

Your ethical compliance education effort will probably have several objectives that focus on communicating expectations, employee responsibility, and organizational resources for making ethical and legal decisions. Table 7-1 lists possible objectives of ethical compliance training. Your objectives will guide the use of specific teaching methods and the content of your education program.

TABLE 7-1
Possible Objectives for Ethics and Legal Compliance Training

1. To communicate an organization's code of conduct and related policies.

2. To communicate organizational responsibility and accountability under the Federal Sentencing Guidelines for Organizations.

3. To ensure employees and agents understand their responsibility for ethical and legal decision making.

4. To help employees and agents recognize ethical and legal issues in the workplace.

5. To empower employees to make decisions based on organizational ethical values and legal standards.

6. To explain the organizational resources devoted to creating and maintaining organizational integrity.

7. To encourage individuals to seek advice and information when unsure of the appropriate organizational response in a situation.

8. To create a culture of honesty and openness in dealing with ethical and legal issues.

Source: Based on authors' knowledge and other sources, including Walter W. Manley, *The Handbook of Good Business Practice* (London: Routledge, 1992).

Training Design and Techniques

In the remainder of this chapter, we offer substantive advice on training design and teaching methods for delivering the strategic integrity message. For more information on general training design and implementation, we suggest contacting your local chapter of the American Society for Training and Development. This professional association sponsors meetings and workshops for understanding the general role of training in organizations. We have found that, especially with ethics, compliance, integrity, and social responsibility, some employees may initially feel awkward about or resistant toward the information. They often believe that these sensitive topics are best left to family and religion and the development of personal ethical values. However, the belief that diverse individuals can independently make the correct ethical and legal decision in a complex organizational context is highly questionable. Consequently, training programs on legal and ethical issues should be designed with several factors in mind.

First, it is important to communicate the differences between personal ethics and organizational integrity. The best training efforts focus on the role of organizational policies and relationships in fostering ethical and legal decision making. Trainers may acknowledge the importance of ethical issues in personal life, but need to articulate that organizational training is designed to clarify work-related decisions.

Second, training that is based only on religion and moral philosophy does not address legal issues from an organizational integrity perspective, nor does it satisfy the FSGO. Although such philosophical discussions may be valuable in employing basic ethical values, organizational training should address specific areas of risk and communicate legal requirements for compliance. Further, a diverse employee base and respect for personal value systems make it very difficult to use theology or a particular moral philosophy as the foundation for training. Organizations need to address issues such as ethical and legal requirements for conducting business on the Internet, discrimination based on various demographic characteristics, and environmental impact requirements. All of these areas have specific legal requirements that cannot be derived from moral philosophy.

Third, training should communicate organizational expectations without moralizing or telling employees what to do in every situation. Effective training programs will increase employees' confidence in making decisions that follow organizational ethics and legal standards.[6] When employees leave the training session, they should feel better prepared and empowered to make the "right" decisions. This preparation will reduce employees' reliance on coworkers in the decision-making process, providing a remedy for potential problems that we discussed in Chapter 3. Training should therefore focus on reasoning skills and employees' capacity for making tough calls.[7] Effective training instills decision-making confidence and an understanding of organizational processes and policies.

Fourth, training should improve employees' understanding of the role that ethical and legal compliance plays in both personal and organizational success.[8] Integrity management must be linked to long-term issues such as customer relationships, job promotion, reputation, profitability, and other accomplishments. In these cases, there may be no substitute for a few stories detailing the effect of the sentencing guidelines and societal expectations on the success (and failure!) of various individuals and organizations.

Fifth, top managers need to play some role in the training effort. Employees will immediately grasp the importance of compliance when upper management's presence is made known during the training. Many companies will feature a president's message on videotape and all training materials. When possible, a personal visit is most effective.' Citicorp is committed to senior managers participating in training sessions with employees because the company recognizes that individuals will only value an initiative when management support is clear.

Sixth, all training efforts should be reinforced in the months following the program. Although all employees should undergo periodic refresher training, your organization can use creative, and perhaps unexpected, methods for reinforcing integrity expectations. Table tents in the cafeteria, messages in paycheck envelopes, internal E-mail bulletins, theme weeks, memo pads, large posters, and other tools have been used to reinforce integrity expectations. Consider the unique approach USF&G Insurance has used. The company has five core values that define its business practices, including teamwork, integrity, innovation, professionalism, and putting the customer first. To keep these values "top of mind," the company's Claim Redemption Center in Florida recognizes at weekly meetings certain employees for living USF&G's core values. The company chooses which individuals to recognize by having employees complete a small card explaining how and why a coworker exemplified one of the core values that week. This relatively low-cost initiative has made the company's core values a real part of employees' expectations for themselves and others on the job. And, it is one of the most anticipated events of the week.

Finally, as with any program, training effectiveness must be periodically evaluated. The FSGO are explicit about the role of continuous improvement in compliance and notwithstanding, employees will appreciate your efforts at subsequent workshops. Your training program must dovetail with ongoing ethical compliance efforts, such as employee surveys, audits, and monitoring the legal environment. Training effectiveness can be assessed for both content and methods of instruction.

Choosing Training Methods

In general, instructional methods in ethical compliance training differ little from those employed in other courses and workshops. However, the sensitive nature of ethics and integrity means that trainers may have to adjust their initial expectations and delivery style. Employees and other participants should recognize both the seriousness of training under the sentencing guidelines for organizations and the role they play in organizational integrity. To accomplish these goals, most trainers will use a combination of approaches listed below. Several studies have suggested that interactive sessions incorporating both company policy and decision-making opportunities are most effective. A manageable number of participants will promote discussion and encourage people to "open up" about their experiences. In its training manual, Lockheed Martin suggests that classes provide plenty of opportunity for discussion by limiting them to fewer than 50 employees.

Lecture and Presentations. The lecture method has been experienced by most (if not all!) employees and trainers as students and has become the preferred method for teaching many subjects. The straight lecture approach creates instructor control, although it is doubtful that trainees will learn very much by simply sitting and listening. The lecture approach is efficient because it can reach a large number of people quickly, and trainees are not required to participate actively in the process. However, lectures and presentations present a few problems for training effectiveness. Employees are usually passive learners in this context, and it is doubtful their decision-making skills will be improved by listening to lectures. Moreover, organizational decision making is the result of both personal and work influences, neither of which can be adequately experienced via passive learning. Finally, most lectures will not expose employees to the myriad of viewpoints that can be taken on ethical issues. The use of short lectures and presentations are usually necessary when an organization introduces its code of conduct and integrity initiatives, as trainees need to understand the background and purpose of the program. Organizations can also use this method to expedite compliance efforts and to set the stage for follow-up training sessions.

Cases and Scenarios. Cases and scenarios can be very good teaching tools for generating discussion among class participants because they incorporate real-life problems and situations. Many organizations, including Tenet Healthcare, are finding the case-analysis method useful for helping employees understand the various personal factors and organizational circumstances that contribute to an ethical or legal di-lemma. With the case method, trainees become active learners because they must read the case, analyze its issues, and make recommenda-tions based on case facts. After the recommendations, the instructor often provides details of the actions taken by actual participants in the case and links participants' recommendations with company policy and industry standards.

Vignettes and short scenarios also provide employees with the op-portunity to engage in decision-making exercises about specific ethical and legal problems. These are relatively brief, typically one paragraph, and place the reader in a situation that requires a decision. Organiza-tions using scenario-based training often develop vignettes that are common in their respective industries. Some scenarios list a number of options from which the reader can choose. These options are useful for making class comparisons, although they force readers into prede-termined responses.

Employees in a training session are usually highly motivated by case studies and vignettes and in many situations, case analyses have been shown to change attitudes.[10] These approaches teach problem solving, although some employees may not be comfortable with the inherent ambiguity. Further, cases and scenarios require the ability to articulate opinions and listen to opposing viewpoints. Despite the importance of case studies and vignettes in communicating ethical compliance, they can be narrowly focused and require little accountability on the read-ers' part. Trainers must balance the strengths and weaknesses of cases, by ensuring that suggested solutions to the issues are realistic under policy, the law, and organizational life.

Role-Playing. The role-playing technique is highly interactive because it requires at least some of the seminar participants to take on the per-spective of an individual caught in a dilemma. In most audiences, there are a few people who will be very willing to participate. The role-play technique can be especially insightful as it elicits the emotions and at-titudes of participants. A perceptive trainer will mentally record the attitudes and emotions portrayed in the role play and provide some mechanism for using them to refine policy and communications.

Video. Most large businesses are using video presentations as one component of their training delivery system. Videos are often used at the beginning and end of seminars for sending an overall corporate message about the importance and scope of ethical compliance. Videos can be used to depict scenarios and cases that are used for group discussion, effectively support many elements of a training program, and add a touch of realism, emotion, and excitement to very serious subject matter. Smaller firms that lack the resources to develop their own videos may be able to obtain them from other sources, such as industry associations or state and federal government agencies. For example, The Massachusetts Commission Against Discrimination (MCAD) offers a low-cost video for small businesses seeking to train employees about sexual harassment. The video examines why sexual harassment is a problem, what it involves, its causes, and resolution. Experts believe that such videos are becoming a necessity for training employees of the "TV Generation" and that trainees are generally positive toward this method because it is fun, action-oriented, and easy to understand. However, we believe videos are best used as a supplement to other training methods and formal communications.

Games. Several companies, including Citicorp, Sony Corporation of American, Wells Fargo Bank, Harris Corporation, and Lockheed Martin, have created organizational games as part of their ethics and compliance education program.[11] As with video, games are an enjoyable means of supplementing other ethical compliance content or testing employees' understanding of company policy and expected practice. For example, Citicorp's "Work Ethic" is a board game that uses hypothetical scenarios and teams to help employees better understand Citicorp's ethics and compliance framework. The teams work through the dilemmas and share their consensus decisions with other workshop participants. In most cases, senior managers are on hand to respond to the teams' decisions and provide the rationale for the company's rules and expectations. Lockheed Martin's *Gray Matters* game has been adopted by over 100 organizations and is very useful for discussing specific ethical dilemmas and the appropriate corporate response. With *Gray Matters,* teams respond to various scenarios and are awarded points based on how well their responses correlate with the best answer as defined by the company. Lockheed Martin recently revised its game, which is now entitled *The Ethics Challenge.* Games, like other training methods, are great for generating discussion, increasing employee involvement, and reinforcing company policy.

Interactive and Computer-Based Training. Advances in technology have made possible a number of training techniques, such as computer-based training, interactive video, and the use of computer intranet systems. Computer-based training is relatively easy to implement in organizations with a large percentage of professional and administrative staff. It provides a high degree of control and consistency because every employee receives the same on-screen messages and explanations. From a compliance training perspective, this is obviously an important feature, especially when employees are required to log in or otherwise record their training time. In addition, computer-based training gives employees great flexibility in fitting the modules into their work schedules. Organizations with field personnel at many locations find computer-based training to be an efficient use of resources. All salespeople at the Intel Corporation carry laptops installed with a compliance training program called "Lawyer in a Laptop."[12]

Interactive training may be computer- or video-based and is designed for employee involvement and decision making, content consistency, and flexibility. GE Aerospace has developed an interactive video program that incorporates scenarios into the training design. Employees work through the scenarios at their own pace and are offered advice and clarification of GE Aerospace policy along the way. The interactive video can be very effective at achieving learning and retention objectives when it is continuously updated and improved. GE Aerospace's program is so successful that it offers the interactive training module free of charge to all companies that have joined the Defense Industry Initiative.[13]

Organizations can also employ their internal computer networks to communicate with employees in diverse locations. Although we know of no attempts to implement wide-scale integrity training in this manner, there are definite possibilities for linking individuals together for decision-making exercises and conflict resolution. The development of "groupware" software allows individuals to work on problems in real time, with input from everyone. The session leader could easily facilitate the process and provide additional exercises for achieving training objectives.

Transferring Training to the Job

Any organizational training effort must be capable of inspiring employees to use the policies and concepts on the job. In terms of ethical compliance training, the ability to transfer an understanding of ethical standards, laws and regulations, and other organizational values to workplace decisions is paramount under the FSGO. Transferring ethics and compliance expectations to work is usually the result of employee characteristics, training design, and the work environment.[14] Your training is only as effective as the decisions that employees make in the following days, months, and years. These decisions may not have legal consequences, but they do affect long-term customer relationships, reputation, community relations, strategic partnerships, and the ultimate success of your organization. As we mentioned at the beginning of the chapter, a carefully designed training program is your organization's best chance for ensuring integrity. As with all employee and organizational development programs, this education should be evaluated for content and later tested against the actions and attitudes of those who completed the training.

TRAINING PROGRAMS TO SUPPORT INTEGRITY MANAGEMENT

We believe that every employee, and director or trustee of your organization should undergo formal training as part of your organizational integrity initiative. A looming question for many firms is whether to train suppliers, distributors, and other nonemployees. Wendy's International has answered that question affirmatively, expanding its integrity efforts to target employees of its franchise owners, even though they technically are not employees of the corporation itself. Wendy's is not liable for the actions of its independent franchisees, nor can it legally force franchise employees to comply with its ethical standards. However, encouraging franchise owners and their employees to adhere to Wendy's integrity standards brings consistency to the franchise and protects the Wendy's name, which benefits everyone.[15]

Many ethical and legal issues involve relationships between employees and nonemployees, and there are a growing number of organizations that evaluate potential partners on both financial and social responsibility measures. Although some organizations may balk at the idea of extending their ethics to others, most of us prefer to work with individuals and firms that we trust to carry out promises and agreements ethically and legally. In the near future, we predict that firms will consciously choose suppliers, distributors, customers and other partners based on a combination of factors, including a strategic focus on implementing organizational integrity. In that case, ethical compliance becomes more than a federally-mandated program—it defines an organization's prospects for the future.

INTEGRITY MANAGER CHECKLIST

Does your organization recognize the importance of implementing training and education programs to communicate ethical and legal standards? If you answer no to many of these questions, your organization needs to reassess its training and educational efforts. A number of yes responses should indicate a concerted effort to disseminate your integrity initiative.

YES   NO

❏   ❏   Does your organization have a formal training program that focuses on ethical compliance?

❏   ❏   Is your formal training program evaluated on a regular basis?

❏   ❏   Does your organization use informal tools for reinforcing its expectations?

❏   ❏   Are your training efforts designed with your employees' responsibilities, job functions, and other characteristics in mind?

❏   ❏   Are your training sessions designed to cover both legal compliance *and* organizational values and integrity?

❏   ❏   Do your education efforts focus on the importance of ethical compliance in organizational success?

❏   ❏   Are top managers involved or in attendance at in-house ethical compliance seminars?

❏   ❏   Do top managers in your organization understand the importance of effective ethics and compliance training programs under the Federal Sentencing Guidelines for Organizations?

❏   ❏   Has your organization implemented or changed its training efforts as a result of the Federal Sentencing Guidelines for Organizations?

❏   ❏   Is the person with oversight for training efforts aware of the "best practices" in ethical compliance in your industry?

CHAPTER EIGHT

MANAGING INTEGRITY IN A GLOBAL ECONOMY

*Overall, the challenge we face is to adapt our global eth-
ics standards to local culture and tradition without compromising our commitment to integrity or abandoning
our competitive advantage.*

> – Keh-Shew Ln, president of Texas Instruments
> Asia, quoted in Ethics Office of Texas Instru-
> ments, *Ethical and Legal Leadership* 200 2
> (June 1996): 2.

As a major U.S. retailer with production facilities scattered around
the globe, the GAP Inc. recognized several years ago that it had a responsibility to monitor these facilities. The company developed a code
of conduct for its overseas contractors and regularly sent employees to
inspect their facilities. So executives were stunned when the retailer came
under attack by the National Labor Committee (NLC), a New-York-
based human rights organization, for human rights violations at an El
Salvador plant that produced clothing for the GAP. According to the
NLC, employees in the Mandarin International factory were forced to
work 12-plus-hour shifts with few breaks in overcrowded and stifling
quarters and were subjected to severe disciplinary action. To draw public attention to the plight of the El Salvadoran workers, the NLC or-
ganized protests in front of GAP stores and a huge media campaign that
resulted in negative publicity for the GAP. The company quickly responded by severing its contract with Mandarin International. Under

pressure from the NLC, the GAP reinstated the contract in order to work to improve working conditions in the plant, reinstate employees fired for union-organizing efforts, and begin independent monitoring. The GAP then announced that it had begun independent monitoring of all its overseas contractors. The retailer also revised its code of conduct and translated it into the native languages of all the countries in which it does business.[1] Many companies, including the GAP and Levi Strauss & Co., have gone to great lengths to ensure that their products are not made by child labor or mistreated workers in their overseas facilities, even when this may be the norm in other countries. However, as the GAP learned, such efforts are no guarantee that ethical and legal issues will not occur, especially when distance, language, and disparate cultural values and customs provide barriers to effective implementation.

Energized by international trade alliances and technological advances, more organizations than ever before are seeking new customers and partners outside their home countries. This globalization has brought together people of different cultures, values, and ethical and legal standards. Consequently, it has become imperative for us not only to understand the values, culture, ethical standards, and laws of our home country, but also to be sensitive to those of other countries.

In this chapter, we consider a number of integrity issues related to the global workplace, with a specific focus on business. We first examine the different perceptions of organizational ethics, cultural differences, and cultural relativism. We also discuss a universal set of ethical principles that is being debated around the world. Finally, we explore some major global ethical issues, such as racial and sexual discrimination, price discrimination, bribery, harmful products, and telecommunications issues. As always, we do not propose to offer absolute solutions to these ethical issues. Rather, our goal is to help you better understand and deal with the complex nature of decisions in a global arena.

CULTURE AS A FACTOR IN BUSINESS

To examine the complexities of decision making in the global arena, we must turn again to the causes of conflict among people and organizations. Obviously, cultural differences among people of different nations provide fertile ground for ethical and legal conflict. These cultural differences stem from language, religion, law, politics, technology, education, social organization, general values, and ethical standards. Each nation has a distinctive culture with its own customs and values, and, consequently, distinctive beliefs and laws about what organizational activities are acceptable. In some cases, European countries set a more stringent standard for compliance than the United States. For instance, comparative advertising in many European countries must be well qualified and documented, or it may be illegal. Even where cultures are similar, marketing and promotional campaigns need to be adapted to each country's laws and ethical standards. Thus, when conducting business across borders, employees are likely to encounter values, beliefs, and ideas that may differ from and even conflict with their own.

Obviously, differences in language complicate international transactions, and problems with translation into another language often make it difficult for employees to express exactly what they mean. Communications blunders can offend or anger others, derail important business transactions, and even damage international business relations. When an American bank was given a 30-day option to purchase a Middle Eastern bank, the American buyer suggested, in French, that the loans be put into an escrow account, a common American practice. However, in French, *escrow* translates to a gyp, or cheater. The local bank officials, insulted and upset, left the negotiating table and ultimately sold the bank to another group.[2] Even differences in body language can lead to misunderstandings. Americans, for instance, nod their heads up and down to indicate "yes," but in Albania this means "no," and in Britain it indicates only that listeners hear, not that they agree. Pointing the index finger, a commonplace gesture among Americans, is considered quite rude in Asia and Africa.[3] Table 8-1 lists examples of gift-giving behavior that may be construed as impolite or even unethical in certain regions of the world.

When firms transfer personnel from one country to another, cultural variations can turn into liabilities. Consequently, large corporations such as IBM and General Motors spend thousands of dollars per family to ensure that the employees they send abroad are culturally prepared. Seemingly innocuous customs of one country can be offensive or even

TABLE 8-1
It's Not the Gift That Counts, but How You Present It

Japan

- Do not open a gift in front of a Japanese counterpart unless asked and do not expect the Japanese to open your gift.

- Avoid ribbons and bows as part of gift wrapping. Bows as we know them are considered unattractive and ribbon colors can have different meanings.

- Do not offer a gift depicting a fox or badger. The fox is the symbol of fertility; the badger, cunning.

Europe

- Avoid red roses and white flowers, even numbers, and the number 13. Do not wrap flowers in paper.

- Do not risk the impression of bribery by spending too much on a gift.

Arab World

- Do not give a gift when you first meet someone. It may be interpreted as a bribe.

- Do not let it appear that you contrived to present the gift when the recipient is alone. It looks bad unless you know the person well. Give the gift in front of others in less personal relationships.

Latin America

- Do not give a gift until after a somewhat personal relationship has developed unless it is given to express appreciation or hospitality.

- Gifts should be given during social encounters, not in the course of business.

- Avoid the colors black and purple; both are associated with the Catholic Lenten season.

China

- Never make an issue of a gift presentation—publicly or privately.

- Gifts should be presented privately, with the exception of collective ceremonial gifts at banquets.

Source: Originally appeared in "International Business Gift-Giving Customs," previously published by the Gillette Company Stationery Products Group. Out of print.

dangerous in others. For example, one GM employee stationed in Kenya invited his managers to a business dinner at a local Nairobi restaurant and invited their wives to attend as well. However, married women in Kenya view restaurants as places frequented by prostitutes and marked by loose morals.[4]

Many companies invest considerable research and effort to try to accommodate local customs and values when doing business abroad. For instance, because eating beef is taboo among India's Hindu population, McDonald's chose to market chicken, fish, and vegetable burgers there instead of beef to avoid giving offense. However, companies are not always so considerate of other cultures' values and mores. One foreign company doing business in the People's Republic of China (PRC) was frustrated by six-month customs delays of advertising materials that included poster maps. It seems that the maps did not include Hong Kong as well as Taiwan (Republic of China), a fact the Chinese customs agents took offense to.[5]

CULTURAL RELATIVISM

When asked how to succeed in China, a senior salesperson from a German firm responded that he regularly pays up to $30,000 in order to get to see a decision maker. A Japanese company reportedly won a $320 million Middle Eastern contract by paying government officials $3 million. And in Indonesia, businesspeople complain that a payment to officials of $1,800 is required to correctly process foreign work permits.[6] "When in Rome do as the Romans," or, "You must adapt to the cultural practices of the country you are in," are explanations many employees offer for straying from their own ethical values when doing business abroad.

When businesspeople defend the payment of bribes or "greasing the wheels of business" and other questionable practices in this fashion, they are resorting to *cultural relativism*—the notion that morality varies from one culture to another because organizational practices are defined as right or wrong by the particular culture. In Japan, for example, the custom has been to discriminate against women in the workplace. In a 1995 survey of female job seekers in Japan, common reasons cited for rejection ranged from gender to judgments about their legs.[7] Cultural relativists would argue that because sexual discrimination is within the Japanese tradition, it is ethical in Japan. Most of us would agree that organizations should obey and respect the legal environment of any country in which they do business. But many managers debate the use of cultural relativism as a global ethics strategy.

Clearly, the question of whose values and ethical standards take precedence in negotiations and business transactions is a major issue in global business. When conducting business outside your own country, should you impose your values, ethical standards, and even laws on members of other cultures? Or should you adapt to the values, ethical standards, and laws of the country in which you are doing business? As with many ethical issues, there are no easy answers to these questions.

A UNIVERSAL SET OF ETHICS

Wouldn't it be great if someone would just establish a set of universal values and ethical standards to apply to international business decision making?! Many people and organizations have tried to do just that: Table 8-2 lists some "universal" values derived from six such efforts. While many would argue that creating a set of universal values is impossible, from Table 8-2 emerges a pattern of shared values— such as truthfulness, integrity, fairness—around the world. Using similar lists derived from sources such as the United Nations Universal Declaration of Human Rights (1948), business ethicist William Frederick developed a Moral Authority of Transnational Corporate Codes, which addresses five areas: employee practices and policies, basic human rights and fundamental freedoms, consumer protection, environmental protection, and political payments and involvement.[8] This global code of conduct is in line with the expectations that many governments have for multinational corporations (MNCs) doing business in their countries. Another noteworthy effort comes from the Caux Round Table in Switzerland, in collaboration with business leaders in Europe, Japan, and the United States. These codes can be accessed on this book's Web site.

The intent of these global codes was to create a common set of acceptable business practices. However, if there is a universal set of ethics, why then do organizations have problems understanding what is ethical and unethical? The answer lies partially in how these basic rights and responsibilities are put into effect. When someone from another culture mentions integrity or democracy, listeners look reassured. However, when these concepts are implemented or practiced on a daily ba-

TABLE 8-2
Global Values

1983 Parliament of the World's Religions *The Declaration of a Global Ethic*	State of California *Handbook on...Moral and Civic Education...*	Michael Josephson *Character Counts, Ethics: Easier Said Than Done*
Nonviolence	Morality	Trustworthiness
Respect for life	Truth	Honesty
Commitment	Justice	Intergrity
Solidarity	Patriotism	Promise keeping
Truthfulness	Self-esteem	Loyalty
Tolerance	Integrity	Respect for others
Equal rights	Empathy	Responsibility
Sexual morality	Exemplary conduct	Fairness
	Reliability	Caring
	Respect for family, property, law	Citizenship
William J. Bennett *The Book of Virtues*	**Thomas Donaldson** *Fundamental International Rights*	**Rushworth W. Kidder** *Shared Values for a Troubled World*
Self-discipline	Physical movement	Love
Compassion	Property, ownership	Truthfulness
Responsibility	No torture	Fairness
Friendship	Fair trial	Freedom
Work	Nondiscrimination	Unity

Source: Andrew Sikula, Sr., *Applied Management Ethics* (Burr Ridge, Ill.: Irwin, 1996), 127. Reprinted by permission.

sis, differences surface. Most cultures value honesty and trust, for example, although each culture may have a different standard or way of gauging these values. In Japan's banking industry, people demonstrate that trust by hiring retired Japanese bureaucrats to become auditors, directors, executives, and presidents, a practice known as *amakudari,* or "descent from heaven." The rationale is that because these men are so trusted, nothing bad or unethical will happen to the banks. The line between regulated and regulator has become blurred because the regulators implicitly trust their former superiors. In the United States, however, businesspeople may trust former superiors, but they also understand that there should always be a line between those who regulate and those who are regulated. In the case of the Japanese, that trust may have been misplaced; the country is now dealing with a $356 billion bad-loan problem, which many believe was caused by these former governmental officials.[9] Although honesty, charity, virtue, and doing good to others may be qualities that are universally agreed on, the differences in evaluating and implementing them can create ethical issues in a global economy.

ETHICAL ISSUES AROUND THE GLOBE

In the remainder of this chapter, we discuss some common issues that arise when companies do business internationally. Major ethical issues that complicate international business activities include sexual and racial discrimination, price discrimination, bribery, harmful products, and telecommunications. This list obviously should not be taken as complete, but represents a sampling of the complex integrity issues that affect decision making in the global arena.

Sexual and Racial Discrimination

Various laws prohibit U.S. businesses from discriminating on the basis of sex, race, religion, or disabilities in their hiring, firing, and promotion decisions. Despite these laws, racial, ethnic, and sexual discrimination remain much-discussed issues in the United States. However, the problem of discrimination is certainly not limited to the United States. In the United Kingdom, East Indians have traditionally been relegated to the lowest-paying, least-desired jobs. Australian aborigines have long been the victims of social and economic discrimination. In many Southeast Asian and Far Eastern countries, employees from particular ethnic backgrounds may not be promoted. Racial discrimination is also apparent in Germany, which will not grant citizenship to Turkish workers, even though some of them are second-generation German residents.

Although women are making inroads into the Japanese business and political arenas, they are seldom promoted to high-level positions. Businesswomen are even more of a rarity in many Middle Eastern nations. Often Middle Eastern women must wear special clothing and cover their faces; in public, they may be physically separated from men. Because many Middle Eastern countries prescribe only nonbusiness roles for women, foreign companies negotiating with Middle Eastern firms have encountered problems with using women sales representatives. Indeed, a Middle Eastern company may refuse to negotiate with a saleswoman or may take an unfavorable view of the foreign company that employs her. The ethical issue in such cases is whether foreign businesses should respect Middle Eastern values and send only men to negotiate sales transactions, thus denying women employees the opportunity to further their careers and contribute to organizational objectives. The alternative would be to try to maintain their own ideas of social equality, knowing that the women sales representatives will probably be unsuccessful because of cultural norms in those societies.

Obviously, discrimination issues are based on deeply held values, social roles, and the unique history and culture of a country. A major problem facing organizations is the potential tradeoff between local expectations and values and the need to foster workplace integrity and achieve business objectives. In the case of gender-based and racial discrimination, some multinationals may have enough opportunities to balance out any potential tradeoffs. For instance, a company with operations in the Middle East and Western Europe may be able to balance its need to promote capable women into high-level positions while respecting the traditional role of women in a particular country. Thus, the firm may consciously raise its number of women executives in Europe to balance the relative lack of them in the Middle East. This is just one example of how an organization can walk the line between its financial goals and integrity objectives. We recognize that this example can be criticized and may not be realistic. However, it demonstrates that discrimination issues require a careful analysis of both organizational objectives and ethical means for reaching them.

Price Discrimination

The pricing of products sold in other countries creates numerous ethical and legal issues. A frequently debated issue in international business is the practice of charging different prices for different groups of customers. Such price differentials are legal in most countries as long as they do not substantially reduce competition or if they can be justified on the basis of costs—for example, the costs of taxes and import fees associated with bringing products into another country. However, price discrimination may be an ethical issue or even illegal if (1) the practice violates either country's laws; (2) the market cannot be segmented; (3) the cost of segmenting the market exceeds the extra revenue from legal price discrimination; or (4) the practice results in extreme customer dissatisfaction. In the United States, the Robinson-Patman Act specifically outlaws price discrimination that harms competition. In other countries, judgments of illegality result from precedent or fairness rulings.

When companies market products outside their own countries, the costs of transportation, taxes, tariffs, and other expenses can raise the prices of the products. However, when the price increase exceeds the costs of these additional expenses, there may be accusations of gouging. Archer Daniels Midland (ADM) Company, which promotes itself as grocer to the world, has been accused of gouging for years. ADM has allegedly been extorting companies who use its high-fructose corn syrup products, which constitute a substantial share of ADM's $11.4 billion a year revenue stream. The U.S. Justice Department's recent assessment of a $100 million fine against ADM for price fixing lends credence to these accusations.[10] Most countries have laws prohibiting companies from charging exorbitant prices for lifesaving products, which include some pharmaceuticals. However, these laws do not apply to products that are not lifesaving, even if they are in great demand and have no substitutes.

On the other side of the coin, companies that charge high prices for products sold in their home markets while selling the same products in foreign markets at low prices which do not cover the costs of exporting the products may be accused of dumping. Dumping raises ethical issues if it damages competition or hurts firms and workers in other countries. It becomes illegal under many international laws if it substantially lessens or reduces competition. Many companies are realizing that dumping is no longer an effective tool, but some have attempted to use other unethical devices such as kickbacks to purchasers, import country assembly, and model-year changes that permit discounting. These strategies are also coming under attack. For example, the EC imposed a $27 to $58 per unit dumping duty on a Japanese firm that assembled and sold electronic typewriters in the EC.[11]

Price fixing is another issue. The United States Justice Department has been actively pursuing those organizations that engage in price fixing. For example, a division of Germany's Bayer AG was charged with colluding with other corporations to eliminate competition in the world market for citric acid between 1991 and 1995. Under the Federal Sentencing Guidelines for Organizations, the company could have been fined between $128 million and $256 million. However, because of the firm's cooperation with the investigation, it was fined $50 million, to be paid out over five years.[12]

Price differentials, gouging, dumping, and price fixing create ethical issues because some groups of consumers have to pay more than a fair price for products. Pricing is certainly a complicated issue in international marketing because of the additional costs imposed by tariffs, taxes, customs fees, and paperwork. Nonetheless, corporations should take care to price their products to recover legitimate expenses and earn a reasonable profit while competing fairly.

Bribery

Bribery is illegal in the United States, but in many other countries, "facilitating payments" are an acceptable business practice. In Mexico, a bribe is called *la mordida,* "the bite," while South Africans know it as *dash.* In the Middle East, India, and Pakistan, *baksheesh,* a tip or gratuity given by a superior, is widely used. The Germans call it *schimengeld,* "grease money," and the Italians call it *bustarella,* "a little envelope." Table 8-3 describes common types of bribes. Companies that do business internationally are aware that bribes are an ethical issue and that the practice is more prevalent in some countries than in others.

Table 8-4 lists several factors that help explain why people give or accept bribes and divides these factors into two categories: home and host country. Many businesspeople view bribes as a necessary cost of conducting business in certain countries. Some executives believe that bribes should be paid if they are the practice in the host country; others disagree. IBM has been accused of providing bribes to Argentinean officials, although it says headquarters knew nothing about them. As one of those under suspicion at IBM commented, "Our honesty was always a tremendous plus and now our reputation for honesty has been destroyed."[13] Once a company starts paying bribes in one country, other countries may expect the same, regardless of the culture.

Since 1977 the U.S. Foreign Corrupt Practices Act (FCPA) has prohibited American firms from offering or providing payments to officials of foreign governments for the purpose of obtaining or retaining business abroad. Companies that violate the FCPA may be fined up to

TABLE 8-3
Major Types of Bribes

Facilitating payments	Disbursements of small amounts in cash or kind as tips or gifts to minor government officials to expedite clearance of shipments, documents, or other routine transactions. Examples: In India, not a single product can move if the clerk's palm is not greased with cash. In Italy, distribution of *bustarella* (an envelope containing a small amount of money) helps to move products into and out of the country more efficiently.
Middlemen commissions	Appointments of middlemen (agents and consultants) to facilitate sales in a nonroutine manner, and payment of excessive allowances and commissions to them, not commensurate with the normal commercial services they perform. Often, the middlemen may request that part or all of their commissions be deposited in a bank in a third country. Example: Northrop Corporation's payment of $30 million in fees to overseas agents and consultants, some of which was used for payoffs to government officials to secure favorable decisions on government procurement of aircraft and military hardware.
Political contributions	Contributions that take the form of extortion because they violate local law and custom. Also payments that, while not illegal, are made with the specific intent of winning favors directly or indirectly. Example: Gulf Oil Corporation's payment of $3 million in 1971 to South Korea's Democratic Republican party under intimidation and threat.
Cash disbursements	Cash payments made to important people through slush funds or in some other way, usually in a third country (e.g., deposit in a Swiss bank) for different reasons, such as to obtain a tax break or a sales contract, or to get preferential treatment over a competitor. Example: United Brands' payment of $2.5 million to Honduran officials for the reduction of export tax on bananas via Swiss bank accounts.

Source: Peter J. LaPlaca, ed., *The New Role of the Marketing Professional* (American Marketing Association), 138-145. Out of print.

$1 million, while their executives face a maximum of five years in prison and/or $10,000 in fines. The FCPA does permit small "grease" payments to foreign ministerial or clerical government employees. Such payments are exempted because of their size and the assumption that they are used to persuade the recipients to perform their normal duties, not to do something critical to the distribution of new goods and services.

One criticism of the FCPA is that although the law was designed to foster fair and equal treatment to all, it places U.S. firms at a disadvan-

TABLE 8-4
Factors Responsible for Bribes

Home Country Factors
- Costs of doing business in certain countries
- An established practice in certain countries, no other way to get around
- Encouragement by Pentagon to buy "influence" to pursue Atlantic Alliance
- Importance of hiring middlemen services in certain countries—to bridge gap between medieval aristocracies and modern corporations
- Increasing competition in international markets
- Pressure from top management to achieve results
- Opportunity to protect undercover operations via Swiss banks

Host Country Factors
- Lure of easy money
- Political involvement in decision making
- Token of appreciation
- Friendly gesture
- Fair "business" deal
- Pressure from vendors

Source: Peter J. LaPlaca, ed., *The New Role of the Marketing Professional* (American Marketing Association), 138-145. Out of print.

tage in the global business arena, as other nations have not imposed such restraints on their companies doing business abroad. For example, if three companies—from the United States, France, and Korea—are bidding on a dam-building project in Egypt, the French and Korean firms could bribe Egyptian officials in their efforts to acquire the contract, but it would be illegal for the American firm to do so. Thus the issue of bribery sets the values of one culture—the U.S. disapproval of bribery—against those of other cultures.

When the FCPA was enacted, the Securities and Exchange Commission (SEC) established a voluntary disclosure program. As a result of the program, more than 400 corporations, including 117 of the *Fortune* 500, reported making more than $300 million in facilitating payments and other types of bribes. In 1988 the Omnibus Trade and Competitiveness (OTC) Act reduced some of the effectiveness of FCPA legislation. For example, it redefined foreign lobbying and facilitating payments in such a way as to reduce companies' risk of violations. The OTC also repealed the Eckhardt Amendment, which had prevented senior managers from using agents or employees as scape-goats when bribes were given. The new act makes prosecution even more difficult, thus decreasing the power and applicability of the FCPA in global business settings. The FCPA and OTC are vague on many areas of conduct, and we recommend competent legal advice in making decisions related to these acts.

Harmful Products

Many governments, particularly in advanced industrialized nations, have banned the sale of certain products that are considered harmful. Nonetheless, some companies continue to sell the products in other countries where their sale remains legal. Examples of such products include some pesticides, such as Velsic Phosvel and 2 4-D, which are suspected carcinogens or mutagens; although it is illegal to sell these products in the United States, they are still sold directly or indirectly to other countries. Some manufacturers of these products argue that, given the food shortages in some nations, the benefits of using the pesticides to increase crop yields outweigh the health risk. Profits are a further motivation, of course.

A similar ethical issue relates to the exportation of tobacco products to less-developed countries. Cigarette sales in the United States are declining in the face of stricter tobacco regulations, mounting evidence that smoking causes a number of illnesses and medical problems, and increasing social stigma. As U.S. sales decline, tobacco companies have stepped up efforts to sell cigarettes and other tobacco products in other countries. The ethical issue becomes whether tobacco marketers should knowingly sell in other countries a product that many in their own country consider harmful. Recent evidence suggests that Brown and Williamson Tobacco Corporation officials were aware years ago of the addictive properties of cigarettes and even revealed that the company had added coumarin (an active compound in rat poison and a lung-specific carcinogen) to pipe tobaccos.[14]

While under fire in the United States, tobacco is viewed more favorably by many consumers in underdeveloped countries. They argue that the tobacco industry provides jobs and stimulates economies and that cigarette consumers enjoy smoking. Many also cite the relatively short life expectancy rates of their people as a reason to discount the health hazards of tobacco. In the long run, however, as industrialization raises the standard of living in less-developed countries, in turn increasing longevity rates, those countries may change their views on tobacco. As people live longer and the health hazards begin to cost both the people and government more in time and money, tobacco will become more of an ethical issue in these nations.

Even traditionally safe and adequately tested products can create ethical issues when a marketer fails to evaluate foreign markets accurately or to maintain adequate responses to health problems associated with their products in certain markets. The classic example involves Nestlé Corporation's marketing of infant formulas, which have been tested as safe when used correctly in the supplemental feeding of infants. When the company introduced its product into African countries as an alternative to breast-feeding, local mothers quickly adopted the product. As time passed, however, infant mortality rates rose dramatically. Investigators found that many mothers could not read and therefore were not correctly following instructions for using the formula. Moreover, the water used for mixing with the powdered formula was often unsafe, and poor mothers also diluted the formula to save money, which reduced the nutritional value of the product. Nestlé was further criticized for its aggressive promotion of the infant formula: The company employed so-called milk nurses to discourage mothers from breast-feeding by portraying the practice as primitive, and to promote Nestlé's infant formulas instead. Under heated pressure from international agencies and boycotts by consumer groups, Nestlé agreed to stop promoting the infant formula; it also revised its product labeling and educational materials to point out the dangers of using the formula incorrectly and the preferability of breast-feeding.[15] Although you are probably familiar with this example, you may not know that the company appears to have reverted to its previous practices after a period of time, and as of 1996 the World Health Organization has renewed the boycott.

Another ethical issue relates to the dumping of waste materials into less-developed countries, particularly when they do not know the contents of the trash. Although Africa and Latin America have banned the trade in trash, China has not. Chinese firms reportedly purchase the garbage to obtain residual metals, plastics, and other useful material, from which it is possible to profit with the benefit of cheap labor. However, when the Jiangsu Province imported such waste, it poisoned the public water supply until a 150-square-kilometer "black tide" passed downriver.[16]

Telecommunications

With the increasing popularity of fax machines, cellular phones, and the Internet, global communication is easier and faster than ever before. Using computer databases, E-mail, and the World Wide Web, we can access information in a matter of seconds instead of weeks. However, this ease of information access brings ethical issues, in part because geographic and political barriers have little significance on the Internet. Consequently, it has become difficult to enforce country-specific laws regulating copyrights, pornography, etc. Walt Disney, H & R Block, and most of the news corporations are already finding it hard to protect their materials. Companies such as Viacom and Time Warner worry that enhanced technology will have an even greater impact on copyright infringement. The motion-picture industry fears that new devices that make digital copies of movies will give rise to some who market the films via the Internet. Paramount Pictures, which owns the *Star Trek* franchise, has tolerated the existence of the hundreds of fan-run Web pages that include Paramount-owned *Star Trek* proprietary materials, such as photos and video and audio clips. However, it recently judged about a dozen sites as having gone too far and threatened legal action. One site, for example, had the entire soundtrack to the movie, *Star Trek: First Contact!*[17]

Questionable financial activities, such as money laundering, have also been spurred by global telecommunications. Money laundering can be legal depending on the countries involved and their interpretations of each other's statutes. A decade ago actual paper currency such as dollars, yen, francs, or pounds would have to be converted by smuggling. Today, drug traffickers and others can move funds to other countries through wire transfers and checks. Money laundering has become so pervasive that when a drug sale is completed in the United States a "controller" auctions the money to "brokers," who bid about 85 cents on the dollar for $10 to $20 million bundles. Brokers have two weeks to return 85 percent of the cash to their clients. In a number of instances, law firms have been employed because of the legal limitations on their records, i.e., attorney-client privilege. One such case in the United States involved a banking and entertainment person, who received a phone call from a cocaine cartel threatening to cut him and his family to pieces unless he cooperated. His testimony helped uncover a $100 million money-laundering scheme and implicated a former law professor.

The speed of global communications has even affected integrity in the fashion industry. "Knockoffs" have always been a problem, with copies often entering the market a few months behind the originals and then by way of a few retailers. Technological advances have accelerated the situation in recent years. For example, a fashion show by the Italian designer Gianni Versace in Milan featured a $1,232 rubberized-silk minidress and a $1,370 pink "safety-pin" dress. However, months before these dresses were made available by the designer, Macy's and other large retailers had already ordered and received look-alikes at less than 25 percent of Versace prices.[18] A photograph taken at a fashion show in Milan or Paris can be faxed overnight to a Hong Kong factory; the next day a sample garment is sent by Federal Express to a New York showroom for retail buyers. Stores order these lower-priced "interpretations" for their own private-label collections and sometimes even display the costlier designer versions at the same time. Because competition in malls is fierce and fashion merchandise is highly perishable, the industry has become very competitive. Some designers are countering these imitations by suing and by bringing out affordable knockoff versions before anyone else can.

The future of workplace integrity in our "global village" depends greatly on your organization's ability to manage both "business" and "cultural" issues. The evolution of global communications both expands and complicates this management responsibility as we are all in the process of learning how to adjust to a potentially real-time economy. Some organizations have been proactive in dealing with issues related to communications and culture in a global economy. As you will see in Chapter 10, Texas Instruments is at the forefront of this movement. This global corporation has created a number of programs that balance the company's need for reaching business objectives with its respect for communications privacy, cultural diversity, and a host of business practices and values. Although this chapter has been more descriptive than prescriptive, we wanted to at least set the stage for thinking about your organization's approach to integrity in a global workplace.

INTEGRITY MANAGER CHECKLIST

The following questions will help you assess the preparedness of your organization to meet the challenges of integrity in a global economy. As with the other checklists in the book, a large number of affirmative responses indicates that your firm is making progress toward incorporating global issues into its standards for conduct.

YES   NO

❏   ❏   Is your organization prepared to deal with conflicts with your own culture's values and legal system?

❏   ❏   Is your organization aware of international codes of conduct, such as the Moral Authority of Transnational Corporate Codes?

❏   ❏   Has your organization integrated some aspects of these global codes of conduct into your current policies and procedures?

❏   ❏   Does your organization have a policy or code for dealing with discrimination in business outside the U.S.?

❏   ❏   Does your firm understand price discrimination and its antitrust issues in the context of both U.S. and other countries' laws?

❏   ❏   Do employees and agents of your organization know how to deal with bribery issues internationally?

❏   ❏   Do employees and agents understand the Foreign Corrupt Practices Act? Does your organization have policies on small "grease" payments?

❏   ❏   Does your firm identify and develop policies on harmful products?

❏   ❏   Do employees and agents understand the ethical or legal ramifications of global communications systems including fax, E-mail, the Internet, and overnight delivery systems?

❏   ❏   Has your firm actively researched the ethical and legal issues that can create significant risk and/or destroy integrity relationships with customers and relevant publics?

CHAPTER NINE

CREATING THE GOOD CITIZEN ORGANIZATION

Enlightened capitalism is the best way of changing society for the better. I think you can trade ethically, be committed to social responsibility, global responsibility, empower your employees without being afraid of them. I think you can rewrite the book on business.

– Anita Roddick, founder, The Body Shop

When Avon Products Inc. sales representatives market cosmetic products door to door, they also bring information about breast cancer. Sales of $2 Avon Breast Cancer Awareness pins and $3 writing pens have helped Avon's Breast Cancer Awareness Crusade raise $16.5 million to fund breast cancer education and early detection services at the community level. The drive has also brought Avon major media exposure and increasing sales. Avon recognizes that breast cancer is a major concern of its target market—women—and that addressing this concern helps build stronger relationships with customers while contributing to society.' Avon's efforts are not unique, but are indicative of a growing awareness by companies that consumers prefer to patronize "good citizen organizations," firms that act responsibly and contribute to society. A recent survey, for example, indicated that nearly 90 percent of consumers surveyed would be more likely to buy from the company with the best reputation for social responsibility when quality, service, and price are equal among competitors.[2]

Although we have thus far focused on ethics and legal compliance in this book, we want to extend these goals into an understanding of good citizenship and social responsibility. Essentially, ethics and legal responsibilities are just two dimensions of social responsibility; there are two others—economic and philanthropic (see Figure 9-1).[3] You are familiar with the basic economic and legal foundations of social responsibility, which require that an organization be profitable (or viable in the case of nonprofit organizations) and operate within the law. These are obvi-

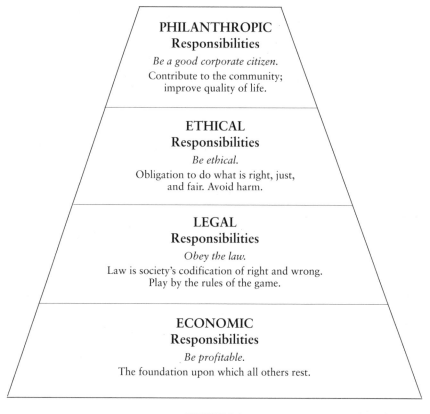

FIGURE 9-1
The Pyramid of Corporate Social Responsibility
Source: Archie B. Carroll, "The Pyramid of Social Responsibility: Toward the Moral Management of Organizational Stakeholders," adaptation of Figure 3, p. 42. Reprinted from *Business Horizons* 34 (July/August 1991). Copyright 1991 by the Foundation for the School of Business at Indiana University. Used with permission.

ously the criteria that define our traditional expectations for organizations. Ethical responsibilities go beyond the law and require organizations to recognize what is right, just, and fair in business activities. Philanthropic responsibilities relate to your organization's contributions to the community and its role within society.

Because these social responsibilities are becoming increasingly important in the decision processes of consumers and other stakeholders, we explore them in this chapter. We also consider what it takes to create a "good citizen organization." This chapter takes a greater external focus than some of the previous ones, as it explores how organizations affect our general society in the long run. If your firm is truly committed to workplace integrity, you will find the following discussion helpful in planning your efforts for citizenship and social responsibility activities.

THE ECONOMIC DIMENSION

At a minimum, business organizations have an economic responsibility to be profitable in order to provide a return on investment for shareholders, provide jobs, contribute goods and services to the economy, and function as members of society. Nonprofit organizations have an obligation to be economically viable in order to fulfill their purpose and goals and contribute to the community. To some readers, the economic level may not seem like a dimension of social responsibility or citizenship. However, we have found that organizations that cannot meet this basic responsibility in the long run often have difficulty moving "up the ladder" to strategic integrity management and good citizenship.

How organizations relate to consumers, employees, stockholders, competitors, the community, and the physical environment affect the economy. The effect of these activities on the economy as it relates to employees is especially significant. Issues include equal job opportunity, workplace diversity, job safety and health, as well as employee privacy. While U.S. laws prohibit discrimination on the basis of gender, race, ethnicity, etc., it seems almost daily that we read about another company settling a racial or sexual discrimination lawsuit. In 1993, the Shoney's restaurant chain settled 20,000 claims for $134.5

million. Since then, Shoney's has become a model of change, with a commitment to hiring minority managers and a better understanding of what went wrong.[4] In fact, many black and Hispanic entrepreneurs have benefitted from a heightened sensitivity toward social responsibility. New businesses such as Colby Care Nurses Inc. and NCS International are creating social good by building wealth for minorities within impoverished communities. Larger companies, such as AT&T, have also created units and programs to benefit diverse community needs as well.[5]

In the U.S., the concept of employment-at-will, which gives companies the right to terminate any employee without just cause, has been used to justify hiring and termination decisions. The trend of corporate downsizing has resulted in the layoffs of millions of employees. Even IBM ended its long-standing no-layoff policy in 1993 in its efforts to improve profitability and competitiveness. The layoffs worked, and IBM is once again competitive and profitable. However, the toll in unemployment from such downsizings creates a tremendous drain on the economy in addition to the personal hardships and suffering that come from being unemployed. Moreover, fears of layoffs can create stress in the workplace, which may contribute to unethical decisions.

Beyond providing jobs and contributing products to the economy, organizations also have a responsibility to compete fairly. Size may give some companies an advantage over others, and large firms can often generate economies of scale that allow them to put smaller firms out of business. Consequently, many small businesses and even whole communities fear the entry of firms such as Wal-Mart and The Home Depot because of their ability to operate at such low costs that small local firms cannot compete. While consumers appreciate the low prices, the failure of small businesses increases unemployment, which places a burden on communities.

Intense economic competition may leave managers feeling that their company's very survival is threatened. They may begin to view normally unacceptable alternatives as acceptable and engage in questionable practices in an effort to ensure the survival of their organizations. Perhaps that's what happened at UTE when it won a contract from the U.S. Defense Department to build Maverick missile launchers. Employees soon realized that the aluminum lugs forged in Germany had cracks and failed to meet the contract specifications. To solve the problem, employees came in on Saturdays when the Defense Department inspectors weren't around, inspected the lugs, then ground the bad lugs to smooth over the cracks before using them to assemble the launchers.[6] While this solution may have addressed the immediate problem, it may create problems with the safety and utility of the Maverick missile launchers. Intense competition may also lead companies to resort to corporate espionage. Espionage is considered an ethical and legal issue because it gives some companies an unfair advantage over competitors and because it sometimes denies the originator of a product or idea the full benefits of having developed it.

Although organizations clearly have an economic obligation to earn a profit for their investors and remain viable for their customers and employers or founders, they must do so within an environment that demonstrates responsibility to society. There are rules of acceptable behavior on which most competitors generally agree. When competitors step over the line of acceptable behavior, legal action may be taken or ethical concerns voiced.

The economic dimension of organizational citizenship is the basis on which the legal, ethical, and philanthropic decisions stand. The economic conditions surrounding any organization will have a profound effect on its goals, strategies, and specific implementation tactics. Just as you have experienced the "highs" of financial success at work, you may also be familiar with the economic pressures that create compromised standards; they often result in ethical and legal issues in the workplace.

THE LEGAL DIMENSION

Laws regulating workplace conduct have been passed because society, including consumers, interest groups, competitors, and legislators, believes that not all organizations can be trusted to do what is right in certain areas, such as consumer safety and environmental protection. This lack of trust is the focal point of the legal dimension. The role of the law is not so much to distinguish what is ethical or unethical as to determine the appropriateness of specific activities or situations. In other words, laws establish the basic ground rules for responsible and ethical work activities. Many of the laws and regulations governing organizational activities fall into one of five groups: (1) regulation of competition, (2) protection of consumers, (3) protection of the environment, (4) promotion of equity and safety, and (5) incentives to encourage organizational compliance programs to deter misconduct. One of the most significant of these is the Federal Sentencing Guidelines for Organizations, which we discussed in Chapter 5.

To illustrate the impact of legislation, consider that American society has responded to research showing that children have difficulties in the use of certain products with special legal protection. For example, it is illegal to market alcoholic beverages and tobacco products to children because our society does not consider these products appropriate for children. Another issue relates to the regulation of television programs and commercials aimed at children. Many people believe that young children are too impressionable to understand and resist today's sophisticated television advertising. These critics view certain types of advertising as irresponsible because they manipulate children's desires. Some critics argue that many children's television shows have crossed the line from true entertainment to marketing messages that encourage children to ask their parents to buy advertised products. In particular, children's programs such as the Power Rangers, Barney and Friends, and The Simpsons have promoted the sale of toys associated with the programs. Other shows have generated controversy by promoting dolls, T-shirts, posters, fan clubs, lunch boxes, and other retail items. The entire entertainment industry is under constant scrutiny for its programming—to the point that it has implemented a variety of ratings systems—but many parents and consumer groups are still not satisfied with their ability to use the ratings systems. Such issues and debates often lead to increased regulation to enforce society's values and desires with regard to children.

Because public policy is dynamic and often changes, many laws have been passed to resolve specific problems and issues. But the opinions of society, as expressed in legislation, can change over time, and different courts, or different state legislatures, may take different views. Laws can help people determine what society believes at a certain point in time, but what is legally wrong today may be perceived as acceptable tomorrow, and vice versa. For example, the Federal Trade Commission is holding hearings and gathering data to better understand marketing on the Internet. The commercial use of the Internet is an evolving area fraught with ethical and potential legal issues, such as unsolicited commercial E-mail, or "spam," the use of "cookies" to monitor consumers' use of World Wide Web pages, and numerous privacy and security issues. By the time you read this, more specific rules and regulation will have been passed to address these issues.

To integrate the legal dimension into an effective workplace integrity program, your organization needs to assess its own legal risk areas, including how specific laws and regulations will affect your operations and activities. You may want to consider developing a matrix, like the sample we have created in Table 9-1, to help assess your firm's specific legal issues. Table 9-1 in no way covers every law that may apply to your organization; such an endeavor would be beyond the scope of this book. However, the matrix can be used as a model for exploring the legal risks inherent in specific departments and activities. This matrix could also be used in training sessions and publications to communicate the specific risks associated with departmental and employee roles. Texas Instruments has used this approach to inform employees of the laws that are most applicable to their respective job functions. How-

TABLE 9-1
Sample Matrix: Laws Affecting the Workplace

		LAWS				
		Sherman Antitrust Act	Foreign Corrupt Practices Act	Environmental Protection Act	False Claims Act	Electronic Communications Privacy Act
FUNCTIONAL AREAS	Human Resources	●				●
	Marketing and Sales	●	●	●		●
	Accounting and Finance	●	●		●	
	Manufacturing			●	●	

ever, the company also tells employees that they should understand their legal responsibilities, even if some laws seem outside the reach of their job duties.[7] In light of the organizational sentencing guidelines, it is imperative that your firm communicate both specific and general laws that affect decision making in your workplace.

THE ETHICAL DIMENSION

Organizational integrity and ethical compliance go beyond obedience to laws and regulations. In fact, managers who define ethics as strict legal compliance may be endorsing ethical mediocrity for their organizations. An effective compliance program must feature integrity as the driving force of the enterprise. While legal compliance is based on avoiding legal sanctions, organizational integrity is founded on guiding values and principles.[8] Good citizen organizations develop these values and principles and do not compromise them to achieve organizational goals. Making ethical principles an important part of a compliance program is more demanding and requires broader and deeper commitment to appropriate conduct. Essentially, a strong ethical culture and compliance program can serve as a buffer to prevent legal misconduct. Figure 9-2 lists some of the ethical components of corporate social responsibility.

Many people question the role of ethics and social responsibility in the workplace. The economic and legal dimensions are generally accepted as the most important determinants of performance. Some economists believe that if firms take care of economic and legal issues, they are satisfying the demands of society and that trying to anticipate and meet ethical and philanthropic needs would be almost impossible. However, many people disagree and believe that organizations must develop appropriate ethics and social responsibility initiatives. A common criticism of business has been that the role of ethics in business strategy has been systematically ignored; however, many organizations have responded by placing ethics at the very center of discussions about business strategy.

1. It is important to perform in a manner consistent with expectations of social norms.

2. It is important to recognize and respect new or evolving ethical norms adopted by society.

3. It is important to prevent ethical norms from being compromised in order to achieve corporate goals.

4. It is important that good corporate citizenship be defined as doing what is expected ethically.

5. It is important to recognize that corporate integrity and ethical behavior go beyond mere compliance with laws and regulations.

FIGURE 9-2

Ethical Components of Corporate Social Responsibility

Source: Archie B. Carroll, "The Pyramid of Social Responsibility: Toward the Moral Management of Organizational Stakeholders," adaptation of Figure 2, p. 41. Reprinted from *Business Horizons* 34 (July/ August 1991). Copyright 1991 by the Foundation for the School of Business at Indiana University. Used with permission.

THE PHILANTHROPIC DIMENSION

Society expects organizations to provide a high standard of living and to protect the general quality of life enjoyed by its members. In addition, organizations are expected to contribute to their local communities. In the past, many organizations made financial contributions in the form of charitable giving and scholarships. Today the trend is toward nonfinancial contributions such as community service and sponsorships of local and national events. Nike, for example, sponsors sporting events at local boys' and girls' clubs and then shows these events in its national advertising. This approach has been called "strategic philanthropy," or financially sound goodwill. Even nonprofit organizations that traditionally have valued and depended on philanthropic generosity also recognize the need to give something back to their communities. Many universities, for example, support initiatives that benefit the community but may be outside the traditional realm of higher education.

Philanthropic efforts in organizations often concern responsibilities to the general welfare of the communities in which they operate. Many firms simply want to make their communities better places for their employees and customers to live and work. The most common way that companies exercise their community responsibility is through donations to local and national charitable organizations. By the mid 1990s, charitable donations by corporations amounted to $6.1 billion, although these donations have declined significantly since 1987 when tax reform and downsizing affected business dramatically.[10] Small businesses often participate by sponsoring charitable events—such as Special Olympics meets or a local March of Dimes Walk-a-Thon—or donating to organizations that support community causes.

Many companies express concern about the quality of education in the United States through philanthropic efforts. Recognizing that today's students are tomorrow's employees and customers, firms such as Kroger, Campbell Soup Company, Eastman Kodak, American Express, Apple Computer, Xerox, and Coca-Cola have donated money, equipment, and employee time to help improve schools in their communities and around the nation. The GE Fund, a nonprofit philanthropic foundation established by General Electric, has provided $20 million for high schools in 14 cities to help improve educational programs.[11] Rather than give cash to causes, some companies donate products. Hewlett Packard prefers donating computer equipment to schools because it is able to deduct its manufacturing costs and build goodwill in relationships with future consumers.[12]

Business is also beginning to take more responsibility for the hard-core unemployed and has created alliances to focus on this problem. Organizations such as the National Alliance of Businessmen fund programs to train the hard-core unemployed so that they can find jobs and support themselves. More companies are beginning to attack this problem, led by the hotel industry. Marriott International, for example, puts welfare recipients through its welfare-to-work program, called Pathways to Independence, which includes training in self-confidence, budgeting and checking-account management, as well as specific job skills. The hotel chain then hires graduates of the program. Says J.W. Marriott, the company's chairman, "We're getting good employees for the long term, but we're also helping these communities. If we don't step up in these inner cities and provide work, they'll never pull out of it."[13] In addition to fostering self-support, such opportunities enhance self-esteem and help people become productive members of society. With changes in U.S. welfare laws, more organizations may have to follow the lead of Marriott and put welfare recipients to work before their benefits expire.

These examples are just the beginning to understanding the philanthropic efforts of organizations. Many of these programs will have only indirect effects on the funding organization—and it may take several years to see this impact. For this reason, organizational citizenship requires a strategic focus that extends the practice of workplace integrity into general social needs and expectations. For many firms, it requires a shift from internal legal and ethical concerns to a concern for the long-term needs of society—most of which will have an influence on employees, customers, government, and all players in the economy. So, being a good citizen organization requires a holistic approach to managing the workplace.

CREATING THE GOOD CITIZEN ORGANIZATION

A "good citizen organization" is both internally and externally focused and integrates itself as an active member of society. While the cornerstone of a good citizen organization is integrity, we believe that it is necessary to become proactive in contributing to the community and society. Table 9-2 provides examples of organizations that have been recognized for their achievements in this area.

TABLE 9-2
Sample of Corporations Recognized for Good Citizenship

Campbell Soup	Johnson & Johnson
Coca-Cola Company	Merck
Adoph Coors Co.	Microsoft Corporation
Corning	Mirage Resorts
Hershey Foods	Procter & Gamble
Herman Miller	

Sources: Dale Kurschner, "The 100 Best Corporate Citizens," *Business Ethics* 10 (May/June 1996): 24-35; Edward A. Robinson, "America's Most Admired Companies," *Fortune*, March 3, 1997, 68-75.

Not all owners, top managers, stockholders, and members of society are comfortable with this proactive role, especially for business organizations. Consider these arguments against a high level of social responsibility and organizational citizenship:

1. It sidetracks managers from the primary objectives of business—profits.

2. Some people question whether business has the expertise needed to assess and make decisions about social problems.

3. Many people believe that social problems are the responsibility of government agencies and officials, who can be held accountable by voters.

There are equally strong arguments for asking business to take responsibility for social issues, including the following:

1. Business contributed to many of the social problems that exist today, so it should play a significant role in solving them—especially in the areas of pollution reduction and toxic waste cleanup.

2. Businesses should be more responsible because they have the financial and technical resources to help solve social problems.

3. As members of society, businesses should do their fair share to help others.

4. Socially responsible decision making by business organizations can prevent increased government regulation.

5. Social responsibility is necessary to ensure economic survival: If companies want skilled, healthy employees, customers with money to spend, and suppliers with high-quality goods and services in years to come, they must take steps to help solve the social and environmental problems that exist today.

Our belief is that the potential benefits far outweigh the negatives associated with organizational citizenship. Obviously, these issues are more relevant in the for-profit sector, as most nonprofit organizations' strategic missions are focused on the welfare of society and quality of life, for at least a small segment of the population. If your firm is committed to many levels of responsibility and supports the philosophy of "community membership," then you are probably acting as a good organizational citizen.

Organizational citizenship also requires an internal focus on economic viability, legal compliance and ethical decision making, coupled with a desire to create beneficial effects on society. In our view, good organizational citizens not only limit their negative effects, but make a concerted effort to benefit the community around them. These benefits should be aligned with the organization's strategic goals and mission, but that does not diminish their importance or contribution. In fact, a strategically sound philanthropic effort usually links back to organizational mission, employees, customers, and local community in a specific way. Recall, for example, that Avon's Breast Cancer Awareness Crusade helps the firm build better relationships with its employees and target market. Just as we, as individual citizens, contribute to society, we also expect to enjoy the results of our contributions and those of others. So organizations often pursue social responsibility activities that will also further their business objectives.

Becoming a good citizen organization may not be a goal to which every reader aspires. Clearly, the most basic priority of economic viability drives many day-to-day decisions at work—and employees who feel pressure at this level may find it easier to disregard the "pie in the sky" philosophy behind ethical and philanthropic behavior. However, on a practical level, the *attempt* to become a good citizen is precisely what the Federal Sentencing Guidelines for Organizations require. We believe the guidelines will become more important and provide an opportunity to improve organizational integrity. Further, it is often a lack of consideration for ethical practices that has led to a number of laws and regulations. So again, top managers should understand that the "self-regulation" accompanying a focus on workplace integrity is actually beneficial in terms of increasing profits and reducing operating costs.

Finally, creating the good citizen organization requires a commitment through both informal attitudes and formal programs. First, top management, employees, and stakeholders must buy into the philosophy that *all* organizations have responsibilities that extend beyond legal and economic obligations. Second, members of the organization must also be willing to explore their beliefs about both workplace ethics and philanthropy. Although these levels of social responsibility are worthwhile, they also require a commitment that can change the way an organization operates. Third, all aspects of social responsibility should be incorporated into the strategic planning process. Most organizations are well versed on the economic and legal aspects, but far fewer have explored how core values and contributions to the community can be aligned with a vision, mission, and strategy. Fourth, the organization must develop a mechanism for assessing its progress in becoming a good citizen organization. We recommend a formal audit that correlates with the annual strategic planning process and general review of your ethical and legal compliance program. The questions that follow in the Integrity Manager Checklist, as well as those in other chapters, provide the basis for an audit to assess the good citizen organization. In the next chapter, you will see some examples of organizations that not only strive to be good organizational citizens, but also clearly link their philanthropic activities to their corporate objectives and mission.

INTEGRITY MANAGER CHECKLIST

Does your organization demonstrate a commitment to good citizenship policies and practices? If you can answer yes to the following questions, your organization both evaluates and monitors its social responsibility, and actively pursues citizenship-focused activity.

YES NO

❑ ❑ Does your organization recognize the economic pressures to engage in unethical or illegal practices?

❑ ❑ Do managers in your firm understand how competition may cause employees to engage in questionable practices?

❑ ❑ Has your organization assessed how its use of technology may have both desirable and undesirable effects on society?

❑ ❑ Is your organization in compliance with antitrust laws and other practices that restrain competition?

❑ ❑ Is your organization in compliance with laws that require businesses to follow health and safety standards for employees and customers?

❑ ❑ Is your organization in compliance with laws that prevent and control pollution and protect the environment?

❑ ❑ Is your organization in compliance with laws that promote equity and safety and prohibit discrimination in the workplace?

❑ ❑ Does your organization have an integrity program to assess its risks and meet the requirements suggested by the Federal Sentencing Guidelines for Organizations?

❑ ❑ Do employees and managers in your organization respect and recognize new and evolving community standards and ethical values?

❑ ❑ Is it important for your organization to achieve its goals without compromising society's ethical norms?

❑ ❑ Has top management in your organization agreed that integrity includes ethical behavior, not just basic compliance with laws and regulations?

❑ ❑ Does your organization contribute resources to the community?

❑ ❑ Does top management believe that your organization should help improve quality of life and the general welfare of society?

CHAPTER TEN

BENEFITING FROM BEST PRACTICES

We hope this book has demonstrated that a strategic focus on workplace integrity is advantageous in many ways in the long run. For further confirmation, just consider the experiences of Hershey Foods, Lockheed Martin, Waste Management, Texas Instruments, and The Home Depot. We're sure their employees, customers, suppliers, vendors, and fellow community members would not have them any other way.

— Debbie Thorne LeClair, O.C. Ferrell, John P. Fraedrich.

Throughout this book we have provided examples of the ethical compliance, social responsibility, and integrity programs of many organizations. Most of these examples have been just a few sentences long and provide only a brief glimpse into excellent policies and programs. In this chapter, we take a more detailed look at the initiatives of five organizations that have demonstrated great commitment, creativity, effectiveness, and success in their efforts. Each organization discussed here stands out, for one reason or another, because it has taken great care to develop, communicate, and continuously refine its approach to workplace integrity. We hope you will be inspired by each firm's commitment and focus on those activities that keep it advancing up the social responsibility pyramid we discussed in Chapter 9, and that you will find useful ideas for creating and improving ethics, compliance, and integrity programs within your own organization. Of course, this list is by no means exhaustive, and we truly welcome your suggestions on organizations with equally admirable approaches. And, we hope your firm will find its place in our next book and chapter on best practices for organizational integrity.

HERSHEY FOODS[1]

Hershey Foods, the number-one confectioner in North America, with sales of nearly $4 billion, exemplifies the power of corporate culture for instilling ethical values and a long tradition of customer *and* employee-centered practices. While most of you are probably familiar with Hershey products such as Hershey's Kisses and Milk Chocolate Bars, Reese's Peanut Butter Cups, and Skinner pasta products, the firm's unique culture may be unknown to some readers, partly because the company makes few attempts to explicitly publicize this particular success. Hershey Foods has been consistently focused on integrity since it was founded by Milton Hershey in the early 1900s. It is often said that the company's founder was more concerned with philanthropy than profits; we say that it was a focus on integrity that created the profitability and longevity of the company.

From the beginning, Milton Hershey was concerned about doing the right thing. He built his firm with high standards of fairness, integrity, honesty, and respect. These standards influenced his relationships with his employees, customers, and community. He put people to work when they were unemployed and did everything possible to treat his employees fairly. During the Great Depression of the 1930s, Hershey hired people to construct a hotel, golf courses, a library, theaters, a museum, a stadium, and other facilities in Hershey, Pennsylvania.

An example of his concern for the community was the founding of an orphanage, the Hershey Industrial School (now called the Milton Hershey School) in 1909. Many of the children who attended the school became Hershey employees, including former Hershey chairman William Dearden (1976-1984). Today, the 10,000-acre school provides education for nearly 1,200 socially disadvantaged children. Although Hershey is now a public company, the school is supported by a trust that owns 42 percent of Hershey Foods. Another example of the company's commitment to youth is its sponsorship of the Hershey's National Track and Field Youth Program. Hershey Foods also supports the Children's Miracle Network, a national program benefitting children's hospitals across the United States. Furthermore, employees may have their gifts to institutions of higher learning doubled via an employee-gift-matching program. Hershey contributes more than $6 million in cash, products, and services to a variety of charities every year.

The strong value system put in place by Milton Hershey remains the guiding philosophy of Hershey Foods today. Whereas some companies hang codes of ethics on the wall or display other outward appearances of ethical standards, Hershey's ethical values are an integral part of the corporate culture. The following statements sum up Hershey Foods' corporate philosophy:

- Honesty, integrity, fairness and respect must be key elements in all dealings with our employees, shareholders, customers, consumers, suppliers and society in general.

- Our operations will be conducted within regulatory guidelines and in a manner that does not adversely affect our environment.

- Employees will be treated with respect, dignity and fairness.

- Our ongoing objective is to provide quality products and services of real value at competitive prices that will also insure an adequate return on investment.

Hershey employees know that their company will support them as long as they focus on quality, integrity, and honesty. Each year the company distributes its "Key Corporate Policies" booklet to all employees to communicate specific policies that provide guidance for handling ethical issues. The booklet consists of the organization's statement of corporate philosophy and policies regarding the use of corporate funds, resources, and conflict of interest; the antitrust law prohibition on price fixing; trading in Hershey Foods and other related securities; and the personal responsibilities of employees. Employees are asked to review the policies carefully, then sign, date, and return a certification card, which states that the employee has read, agrees with, and will abide by Hershey Foods Corporation's "Key Corporate Policies."

Hershey employees who have questions concerning proper policy or conduct are instructed to consult their supervisor first, but they have alternatives if the supervisor is deemed a problem. Antitrust questions are referred to the legal department. Questions about ownership or stock purchases are directed to the corporate secretary's office. The human resources office handles personnel problems. Employees also have the right to go to any corporate or division officer. In addition, employees can call an 800 number to leave a message about any of their concerns.

The company values employee cultural diversity and is able to attract and retain the most qualified employees. Hershey is a corporate sponsor of the National Minority Supplier Development Council, which seeks to expand business opportunities for minority-owned businesses. The company was also recently cited for an innovative program to promote healthier employee lifestyles.

Ethics and social responsibility are not just buzz words at Hershey; they are important ingredients in its corporate culture and how business is conducted on a daily basis. All managers go through ethics-training programs to ensure that they understand how to handle the many complex issues they face in operating the company. Employees have a clear idea of the company's ethical values and know they will be supported in following them. The company continues to be the most profitable company in the confectionery market; it has outperformed the stock market over the last ten years.

LOCKHEED MARTIN[2]

When Martin Marietta and the Lockheed Corporation merged in 1995 to form Lockheed Martin, both companies had a history of problems *and* concerted attempts at managing workplace integrity. As one of the world's largest defense contractors, with global sales of nearly $27 billion, Lockheed Martin faces intense competition to obtain long-term multibillion dollar contracts with complex specifications for high-tech military equipment. In an industry rife with opportunities for misconduct—and enough million-dollar fines and negative publicity to indicate that such opportunities have not always been ignored—Lockheed Martin has come to recognize the importance of integrity as a strategic objective. Lockheed Martin has been very active in the Defense Industry Initiative (DII) and other ethics associations. The company devotes enormous resources to its integrity effort, and quite frequently sets the standard for training and implementation strategies. This worldwide corporation has an extensive network of ethics and compliance officers who are very active in training efforts and other communications. The company has even developed ethics materials for use in other contexts, including high schools.

Today, Lockheed Martin's ethics and compliance program is based on six basic virtues—honesty, integrity, respect, trust, responsibility, and citizenship—which drive all aspects of Lockheed's operating and strategic policy. To communicate these virtues, the company has embraced the ethics officer role as paramount to its "Setting the Standard" corporate compliance program. Further, the company utilizes unique training methods and an aggressive auditing function to continuously improve its ethics and business conduct initiative.

One of the most unique aspects of Lockheed Martin's corporate compliance program involves the level of resources and commitment that top management has provided to the program. In 1996, Lockheed Martin trained more than 190,000 employees and consultants worldwide and investigated over 2,000 ethics cases across the corporation. Many of these cases originated as phone calls to the firm's Ethics HelpLine or ethics officers. HelpLine callers also sought guidance or clarification before they acted on behalf of the company. Lockheed Martin believes that a substantial reduction in anonymous calls, compared to those cases where callers have identified themselves, signifies that employees are developing a greater trust for the company's intentions on ethical and legal decision making.

In recent years, the company has deployed more than 1,000 state-of-the-art digital workstations to 337 company locations, so that employees can utilize 21 different computer/interactive ethics training modules. These modules allow users to work through a variety of compliance-related issues and associated company policies. One module, for example, focuses on the ethical decision-making process and allows users to refine their understanding of how Lockheed Martin wants them to evaluate and respond to ethical issues. The company's *Gray Matters* board game, widely used by many organizations, has recently been transformed into *The Ethics Challenge.*

Finally, the Office of Ethics and Business Conduct at Lockheed Martin is committed to the audit and continuous improvement of its corporate compliance program. About every two years, the company conducts a survey to assess its effectiveness on ethics and compliance issues. In some cases, the survey findings are compared to publicly available results for other organizations and industries, so that Lockheed Martin can continue to set the standard for ethical compliance. The results are also used in future planning efforts designed to improve the company's corporate compliance program. In addition, an external auditor recently found that the company's ethics communications are rated more highly and favorably than any other aspect of Lockheed Martin's internal communications. To the Office of Ethics and Business Conduct, this result indicates that it is getting employees' attention through various communication efforts on its commitment to workplace integrity. From this analysis and other independent opinions, this brief description of Lockheed Martin's programs cannot adequately account for the company's progress and prestige in terms of workplace integrity. In any case, we have great faith in the company's efforts and believe its integrity efforts are well intentioned, well funded, and highly supported by the organization.

WASTE MANAGEMENT, INC.[3]

When Dean L. Buntrock and H. Wayne Huizenga joined forces in 1971 to launch a small garbage collection service, they could not have foreseen that Waste Management Inc. would grow into the world's largest solid waste and disposal company, with sales in excess of $9 billion. Concern over air quality in the 1960s and the subsequent ban of onsite waste burning fueled rapid growth of the waste-disposal industry. In its first year of operations, Waste Management had revenues of nearly $17 million and customers in Florida, Illinois, Indiana, Minnesota, Ohio, and Wisconsin. With Waste Management's success under his belt, Wayne Huizenga left the company for other business pursuits (most notably, Blockbuster Video). Dean Buntrock remained as CEO. The company now employs more than 63,000 people and operates in 20 countries, including Argentina, Venezuela, Australia,

New Zealand, Germany, Italy, France, Finland, and the Netherlands. It has expanded into the only full-line global company offering services ranging from environmental consulting design and engineering to management and disposal, and has controlling interest in four other public companies.

Since Waste Management Inc. was fined $2 million for violation of antitrust laws and $12.5 million for pollution ordinance infringements several years ago, the company has become increasingly concerned with environmental and ethical business practices. The company has made a number of strides in the environmental area and is actively pursuing a workplace integrity effort.

Waste Management's success in improving the organization's ethical decisions is partly due to its code of ethics. Its code of ethics booklet, "Ethics in Our Workplace: Guidelines for Our People," outlines what the company expects from its employees when they are faced with ethical issues. The four-page booklet reminds employees that fairness, honesty, integrity, and trust shape both individuals' behaviors and the company's reputation. It defines what "ethics" means and specifically identifies what is ethical and what is unethical. "Treating values such as fairness, honesty, integrity, and trust as ground rules, not options, in making decisions" is ethical, while "misrepresenting the facts" to a customer, "bad-mouthing the competition," "doing shoddy work," "promising more than we can deliver," and "conspiring to 'cover-up' illegal or unethical customer activities" are unethical.

The code also provides information concerning how to recognize an ethical problem in day-to-day activities in the workplace. It supplies a set of rules to follow and establishes principles to consider when a situation is not specifically addressed. The activities covered range from those with customers, suppliers, and government regulators to dealings with fellow employees and competitors. Waste Management makes the information easy to follow and understand through the use of cartoons, pictures, and short moral quotes sprinkled throughout the pamphlet.

The booklet also outlines what to do and whom to contact when faced with a moral dilemma at work. The employee, who may remain anonymous, is provided a toll-free telephone Helpline number and guaranteed to be "treated with respect and dignity." Anyone in a position of authority over the employee is subject to disciplinary action or dismissal if an attempt is made to harass or stop the employee from using the Helpline. Concerns also may be submitted by fax, letter, or E-mail.

Ethics training at Waste Management is designed to help employees recognize ethical issues and make ethical choices well above the standards set for legal compliance. Through ethical leadership and group problem resolution, employees practice recognizing ethical issues and improving decisions. Training includes the use of a videotape which presents ethical situations commonly faced by Waste Management employees. Dealings with outside vendors, fellow workers, and supervisors are played out in settings with which employees are familiar. One such vignette features a project manager facing pressure from her general manager to falsify test reports to a government agency about the project. The tests had been run to determine how well the lining of a new dump site would contain chemical waste. Though several successful tests had been conducted, weather may have caused weaknesses in areas of the lining which had already been tested. Reworking the areas would cause the project to be finished late and over budget. Under pressure to come in on time and under budget, the general manager tells the project manager to finish the project and turn in the successful reports. As the scene fades, the project manager turns to the camera and asks, "What would you do?" Faced with the possibility of being fired for disobeying her supervisor, what should she do?

Providing such vignettes and case studies in employee training sessions stimulates discussion about what the most ethical action might be. However, just as we have repeatedly emphasized, Waste Management recognizes that ethics training is only a part of an overall ethics program. It must be supported by top management and tools such as the code of ethics and video presentations. Tools alone, however, are not sufficient. If a program is to be effective, it must be enforced.

Waste Management's efforts to improve workplace integrity have not gone unnoticed. As evidence of its success in implementing ethical and environmental practices, the Occupational Safety and Health Administration (OSHA) currently uses a facility of one of its subsidiaries, Chemical Waste Management, as a model for addressing recent safety laws through good faith efforts in compliance. Waste Management's strong ethics training program and the supportive philosophy adopted by its management has improved the firm's reputation for being socially responsible and has resulted in a better relationship with government agencies.

TEXAS INSTRUMENTS[4]

Texas Instruments (TI) is one of the world's foremost high-tech companies, with $10 billion in sales and operations in more than 30 countries. TI products and services range from semiconductors to defense systems to consumer electronic products. Since its birth in the early 1930s, TI has been a pioneer in many technologies, including transistor radios, calculators, and integrated circuits. The company strives for excellence by following principles based on ethics, integrity, total quality management, good corporate citizenship, and other business-related goals. To achieve these goals, TI has created a comprehensive ethical compliance program that incorporates technology and global concerns with great sophistication. The company manages its ethics expectations and legal compliance by balancing local culture with the cornerstones of TI's overall business philosophy.

TI has had a code of conduct since 1961, making its ethics initiative one of historical significance. The company's code addresses issues relating to policies and procedures; government laws and regulations; relationships with customers, suppliers, and competitors; gifts and entertainment; political contributions; business payments; conflicts of interest; investment in TI stock; handling of proprietary information and trade secrets; relationships with government officials and agencies; and enforcement of the code. TI's code emphasizes that ethical behavior is critical to maintaining a profitable enterprise:

> The trust and respect of all people—fellow workers, customers, stockholders, government employees, elected officials, suppliers, competitors, neighbors, friends, the media, and the general public—are assets that cannot be purchased. They must be earned every day. This is why all of TI's business must be conducted according to the highest ethical, moral, and legal standards.

Acknowledging the vital role that communications plays in any compliance initiative, TI has developed a variety of brochures, newsletters, and booklets that serve as practical reminders on ethical and legal issues. The foundation of this communication effort is a booklet called "Cornerstone," which uses a question-and-answer format to explore a number of possible ethical issues and how employees should resolve them. The booklet provides a toll-free number for employees to call, anonymously, to report incidents of unethical behavior or simply to ask questions. The "Cornerstone" publication also includes an "ethics quick test" to help employees when they have doubts about the ethics of specific situations and behaviors:

- Is the action legal?

- Does it comply with our values?

- If you do it, will you feel bad?

- How will it look in the newspaper?

- If you know it's wrong, don't do it!

- If you're not sure, ask.

- Keep asking until you get an answer.

Because of its products and markets, Texas Instruments often finds itself on the cutting edge of potential ethical and legal issues. Other company publications therefore address issues ranging from product safety to use of the Internet. For example, its booklet, "The Networked Society," offers advice on using Internet resources, by exploring a variety of situations that employees are likely to encounter and providing some remedies for tough situations.

Another pamphlet, "Working Globally," focuses on the complexities of conducting business legally and ethically in over 30 countries around the world. TI has managed its ethics program so that it is applicable in many cultures by implementing it as "global strategy, locally deployed." Although the company has a core set of values, local managers are given the responsibility of carrying out these values by utilizing a three-part approach. First, they are expected to ask, "Are we complying with all local laws?" Second, they ask, "Are there business practices at the local level which impact how we interact with coworkers in other parts of the world?" And finally, they ask, "Do some of our practices need to be adapted based on the local laws and customs of a specific location?"

Texas Instruments' approach to workplace integrity, just like Lockheed Martin's, has the unwavering support of top management. This support is evident in the resources devoted to ethics—or what TI calls the cornerstone of its business. We also believe that the TI Ethics Office is innovative and one of the most respected in the world. After all, the company has been leading the charge for ethical business conduct for nearly four decades.

HOME DEPOT [5]

The Home Depot is well known for its do-it-yourself marketing success, although the company is just as focused on social responsibility and good corporate citizenship. The company has found many ways to link its core business to community needs. But given its history, management style, and ability to meet objectives, the company has also been a great place for most employees and investors alike.

The Home Depot was founded in 1978 by Bernard Marcus, Arthur Blank, and Ronald Brill, who each had previous experience in the do-it-yourself and home improvement markets. Today, the company is the largest home center retailer in North America, with nearly 500 stores and sales in excess of $19 billion. The Home Depot has found a simple recipe for success—take the service and convenience of a small hardware store and provide it in a location about the size of an airplane hangar. The company augments its service and merchandising strategy with a corporate culture that values decentralized management, entrepreneurial innovation, and high levels of employee commitment and enthusiasm. This strategy has earned The Home Depot *Fortune's* top spot as the U.S.'s most admired retailer for several years running.

The Home Depot takes "responsible retailing" very seriously. This responsibility extends to a number of stakeholders, including employees, customers, vendors, communities, and the environment. The company has been commended in Canada for its ethics training workshops and overall belief that when "employees believe in the ethical correctness of their workplace arrangements, their employer gains their support and loyalty." The Home Depot encourages its customers to purchase "green" products and to recognize the potential environmental effects of do-it-yourself projects. After projects are complete, customers can bring their waste materials to recycling centers at Home Depot stores, and the company will dispose or recycle the waste appropriately. Vendors are also carefully scrutinized for their commitment to human rights and non-exploitative practices and are required to meet specific guidelines for environmental consciousness.

The Home Depot is also highly committed to employing individuals with varied backgrounds and abilities through its "Different Shades of Orange." The company has been recognized by the Association of Retarded Citizens and the Western Law Center for Disability Rights for its hiring practices. To demonstrate its concern for the well-being of all employees, the company created the program, "Building a Better Health," which includes opportunities for employees to learn more about general health, prevention, and overall fitness. This program also includes a special module for expectant mothers that has worked to decrease premature births and overall health care expenses.

In a serious effort to infuse surrounding communities with donations and "free labor" from its employees, The Home Depot's main philanthropic efforts are focused on at-risk youth and affordable housing. The main driver behind the success of its philanthropic efforts is the fact that The Home Depot supports and provides services that relate to its core business. For this reason, Habitat for Humanity, Earth Day, and other related programs are highly valued by the company.

The Home Depot has done an excellent job of aligning its philanthropic efforts with its overall corporate mission. New employees are socialized into a culture that values participation on many levels—at work and in the community. We encourage you to watch as the company grows, matures, learns, and hopefully, continues to increase its social responsibility efforts.

USING BEST PRACTICES FOR INTEGRITY MANAGEMENT

The companies cited in this chapter have made the crucial step from writing policy to implementing strategies and corporate cultures that foster integrity. Under the FSGO, this is obviously an imperative step. From the broader perspective of integrity-based management, the ability to effectively instill an ethical culture is a time-consuming, often difficult, and never-ending process. Chapter 7 described training techniques that can be used to facilitate this process and communicate your integrity standards. Additionally, we have found that most organizations with ethics initiatives are quite willing to share their ideas. Several industries are actively involved in sharing information on best practices. Representatives from the telecommunications industry, for example, meet regularly to discuss compliance and ethics issues. To guard against antitrust problems, the group includes antitrust attorneys as participants and maintains minutes of the meetings. The telecommunications companies are careful to share information about their respective integrity initiatives, but do not attempt to set industry practice. These forums have been very successful at helping members become more knowledgeable, better prepared, and confident about their companies' integrity programs.[6] So don't hesitate to call others if your goal is to better understand how to improve ethical decision making in your organization, not just to establish the lowest common denominator of legal compliance.

The organizations that we have highlighted in this chapter and throughout the book are unique for their commitment to workplace integrity and, more importantly, for their willingness to acknowledge the influence of organizational culture, top management, policies, and coworkers on daily ethical and legal decisions. Essentially, top management in these companies has made workplace integrity a strategic priority—not just a tactic to meet the Federal Sentencing Guidelines for Organizations or to appeal to public relations pressures. While some organizations start out with the legalistic approach, those most effective at managing long-term integrity move beyond this perspective into their own unique way for encouraging ethical decision making. And those employees, managers, and other organizational members focused on ethics will probably make fewer decisions that create legal problems. However, as any good ethics officer will tell you, no program or system for managing ethical and legal decisions is perfect. The companies named in this chapter, and many of the ones listed throughout this book, have also had ethical and legal issues to address. As this book was going to print, for example, we learned that Home Depot faces allegations of sexual discrimination. These charges, which the company vehemently denies, will now be tested in a civil courtroom.[7] Regardless of the outcome of these cases, we believe that The Home Depot's commitment to continuous improvement of its integrity program will contribute to organizational learning and help to build an even stronger ethical climate.

We hope that this chapter and the rest of the book have inspired you to reconsider and evaluate your organization's approach to workplace integrity. Although legal compliance issues may be driving a great deal of the current focus on ethics in the workplace, many organizations are convinced that integrity is good business. One question we are often asked is whether there really is an empirical link between integrity initiatives and profitability. To date, the results are mixed—some showing a positive relationship between financial performance and social responsibility, others not showing a relationship at all.[8] However, we know of a number of ways that integrity does correlate with financial performance, such as customer retention, positive word-of-mouth communications, employee commitment and retention, general trust in work relationships, fewer legal problems, and perhaps, the reduction of government regulation. A recent article in *Business Ethics* highlighted five best practices that can lead to improved financial performance. These practices include: 1) progressive workplace practices, such as open management styles and employee assistance programs, that reduce turnover; 2) support of causes that people find important, which may encourage customers to switch to your brand or organization; 3) aggressive environmental practices that help ethical organizations outperform "high polluters" 80 percent of the time; 4) sincere community ties that create stronger employee and customer commitment; and 5) employee ownership that keeps high quality employees with your organization.[9]

These practices, as well as those initiated by organizations mentioned throughout the book, are indicative of the integrity-based management approach that we have advocated since Chapter 1. Although the empirical evidence for the "profitability" of workplace integrity is still in progress, most managers, owners, and employees want to make decisions that improve the ethical nature of work, business, and societal relations. We hope this book has demonstrated that a strategic focus on workplace integrity is advantageous in many ways in the long run. But, if our word is not enough, just consider the experience of Hershey Foods, Lockheed Martin, Waste Management, Texas Instruments, and The Home Depot. We're sure that their employees, customers, suppliers, and fellow community members would not have it any other way.

Integrity Manager Checklist

The following questions are based on the experiences of the companies we discussed in this chapter. In general, if you answer no to many of these questions, your organization needs to evaluate its commitment to workplace integrity and its related policies and programs for ensuring ethical compliance.

YES NO

❏ ❏ Do employees know the ethics and legal compliance history of your organization?

❏ ❏ Do suppliers and customers recognize your organization's stand on ethics and legal compliance?

❏ ❏ Are you familiar with the integrity initiatives of other organizations in your industry?

❏ ❏ Are you aware of the best practices in ethical compliance, regardless of industry?

❏ ❏ Has your organization sought guidance on its ethics and compliance efforts from others?

❏ ❏ Does your organization show a commitment to integrity throught its allocation of resources?

❏ ❏ If applicable, does your firm reconcile the need for consistent organizational ethical values with different cultural beliefs in other parts of the world?

❏ ❏ Are your organization's philanthropic efforts aligned with its overall strategic mission?

❏ ❏ Has your organization compared its integrity initiative with those of other firms?

ENDNOTES

Chapter 1

1. "Ethics Poll Answer: The Company Made Me Do It," *St. Petersburg Times*, August 26, 1996, 14.

2. "Ethics Poll Answer."

3. "Does It Pay to Be Ethical?" *Business Ethics* 11 (March/April 1997): 14-15.

4. Dale Kurschner, "5 Ways Ethical Busine$$ Creates Fatter Profit$," *Business Ethics* 10 (March/April 1996): 20-23.

5. Mark Maremont, "Blind Ambition," *Business Week*, October 23, 1995, 78-92.

6. Terry W. Loe and O.C. Ferrell, "Ethical Climate's Relationship to Trust, Market Orientation, and Commitment to Quality: A Single Firm Study," Academy of Marketing Science annual conference, May 1997.

7. Alan R. Yuspeh, "Development of Corporate Compliance Programs: Lessons Learned from the DII Experience," in *Corporate Crime in America: Strengthening the "Good Citizen" Corporation* (Washington, D.C.: U.S. Sentencing Commission, 1995), 71-79.

8. Eleanor Hill, "Coordinating Enforcement Under the Department of Defense Voluntary Disclosure Program," in *Corporate Crime in America: Strengthening the "Good Citizen" Corporation* (Washington, D.C.: U.S. Sentencing Commission, 1995), 287-294.

9. Richard P. Conaboy, "Corporate Crime in America: Strengthening the Good Citizen Corporation," in *Corporate Crime in America: Strengthening the "Good Citizen" Corporation* (Washington, D.C.: U.S. Sentencing Commission, 1995), 1-2.

10. *United States Code Service* (Lawyers Edition), 18 U.S.C.S. Appendix Sentencing Guidelines for the United States Courts (Rochester, NY: Lawyers Cooperative Publishing, 1995) 8A.1.

11. Conaboy, "Corporate Crime," 1.

12. "Ethics Training Is Big Business," *St. Petersburg Times*, August 26, 1996, 15.

13. Mark Hendricks, "Ethics in Action," *Management Review* 84 (January 1995): 53.

14. Hendricks, "Ethics in Action."

Chapter 2

1. G. Pascal Zachary, "Bags of Trouble: Korean Grocer Learns the Law Doesn't Care About His Good Deeds," *The Wall Street Journal*, July 30, 1996, A1, A9.

2. *Ethics in American Business: Policies, Programs and Perceptions* (Washington, D.C.: Ethics Resource Center, 1994).

3. "Ethics Poll Answer: The Company Made Me Do It," *St. Petersburg Times*, August 26, 1996, 14.

4. Vernon R. Loucks, Jr., "A CEO Looks at Ethics," *Business Horizons* 30 (March-April 1987): 4.

5. Steve Stecklow, "Cheat Sheets: Colleges Inflate SAT's and Graduation Rates in Popular Guidebooks," *The Wall Street Journal*, April 5, 1995, A1, A4.

6. Eric H. Beversluis, "Is There 'No Such Thing as Business Ethics'?" *Journal of Business Ethics* 6 (February 1987): 81-88. Reprinted by permission of Kluwer Academic Publishers, Dordrecht, Holland.

7. Beversluis, 82.

8. Glenn R. Simpson, "Exxon Advertising

Claims of 'Clean Gas' Are Challenged in Complaint by FTC," *The Wall Street Journal,* September 18, 1996, A4.

9. Alix M. Freedman and Suein L. Hwang, "Why Don't Low-Tar Cigarettes Have Lower Nicotine?" *The Wall Street Journal,* July 14, 1995, A1.

10. Archie B. Carroll, *Business and Society: Ethics and Stakeholder Management* (Cincinnati: South-Western, 1989), 228-230.

11. *Dateline NBC,* report on Louisiana law enforcement agencies, aired on Friday, January 3, 1997.

12. "Cut Down: Timber Town Is Bitter over Efforts to Save the Rare Spotted Owl," *The Wall Street Journal,* January 6, 1992, A1, A8.

13. Dean Starkman, "Compliance Ruling May Shield Directors," *The Wall Street Journal,* December 24, 1996, B5.

14. Suein L. Hwang, "The Executive Who Told Tobacco's Secrets," *The Wall Street Journal,* November 28, 1995, B1, B6.

15. Andy Pasztor, "Hughes Aircraft Pays $4.5 Million to Settle False-Testing Lawsuit," *The Wall Street Journal,* September 11, 1996, B7.

16. William M. Carley, "Rigging Computers for Fraud or Malice Is Often an Inside Job," *The Wall Street Journal,* August 27, 1992, A1, A4.

17. Carley, "Rigging Computers for Fraud or Malice Is Often an Inside Job."

18. Andy Pasztor, "Probe of Rockwell Unit Expands; Hazardous Waste Disposal at Issue," *The Wall Street Journal,* December 21, 1995, B7.

19. Scott McCartney, "Compaq Suit Claims Packard Bell Sells New Computers Containing Used Parts," *The Wall Street Journal,* April 11, 1995, A2.

20. Thomas M. Buton, "Dow's Role in Implants Is Given New Light," *The Wall Street Journal,* December 21, 1994, B4.

21. "Doctor Assails J&J Price Tag on Cancer Drug," *The Wall Street Journal,* May 20, 1992, B1, B8.

22. Paul Raeburn, "Magazine Spread Tobacco Views to Kids, Study Says," *The Commercial Appeal,* November 1, 1995, B6.

23. Matt Murray, "Former Phar-Mor President Guilty in Fraud Case," *The Wall Street Journal,* May 26, 1995, B1.

24. Lee Berton, "Code May Force CPAs to Inform on Employees," *The Wall Street Journal,* August 4, 1995, B4, B12.

25. Timothy L. O'Brien, "Law Firm's Downfall Exposes New Methods of Money Laundering," *The Wall Street Journal,* May 26, 1995, A1, A6.

26. TECO Energy, Inc. *History of TECO Energy's Commitment to Ethical Standards and Legal Compliance,* 1993, Tampa, FL.

Chapter 3

1. "ADM Admits Guilt in Price-Fixing," *The Tampa Tribune,* October 15, 1996, Business/Finance section, 1, 8; Ronald Henkoff, "So Who Is This Mark Whitacre, and Why Is He Saying These Things About ADM?" *Fortune,* September 4, 1995, 64-68; and Mark Whitacre and Ronald Henkoff, "My Life as a Corporate Mole for the FBI," *Fortune,* September 4, 1995, 52-62.

2. O.C. Ferrell and Larry G. Gresham, "A Contingency Framework for Understanding Ethical Decision Making in Marketing," *Journal of Marketing* 49 (Summer 1985): 87-96; O.C. Ferrell, Larry G. Gresham, and John Fraedrich, "A Synthesis of Ethical Decision Models for Marketing," *Journal of Macromarketing* 9 (Fall 1989): 55-64; Shelby D. Hunt and Scott Vitell," A General Theory of Marketing Ethics," *Journal of Macromarketing* 6 (Spring 1986): 5-16; Thomas M. Jones, "Ethical Decision Making by Individuals in Organizations: An Issue-Contingent Model," *Academy of Management Review* 16 (February 1991): 366-395; William A. Kahn, "Toward an Agenda for Business Ethics Research," *Academy of Management Review* 15 (April 1990): 311-328; and Linda K. Trevino, "Ethical Decision

Making in Organizations: A Person-Situation Interactionist Model," *Academy of Management Review* 11 (March 1986): 601-617.

3. Jones, "Ethical Decision Making by Individuals in Organizations," 367, 372.

4. Donald P. Robin, R. Eric Reidenbach, and P.J. Forrest, "The Perceived Importance of an Ethical Issue as an Influence on the Ethical Decision-Making of Ad Managers," *Journal of Business Research* 35 (January 1996): 17.

5. Robin, Reidenbach, and Forrest, "The Perceived Importance of an Ethical Issue."

6. Jay Koblenz, "Avoiding Dealer Discrimination," *Black Enterprise*, November 1995, 177.

7. Del Jones, "Denny's Faces Another Claim of Racial Bias," *USA Today*, September 28, 1995, B1.

8. Robin, Reidenbach, and Forest, 17.

9. F. Neil Brady, *Ethical Managing: Rules and Results* (New York: Macmillan, 1990), 4-6.

10. Lawrence Kohlberg, "Stage and Sequence: The Cognitive Developmental Approach to Socialization," in *Handbook of Socialization Theory and Research*, ed. D.A. Goslin (Chicago: Rand McNally, 1969), 347-480.

11. Kohlberg, "Stage and Sequence: The Cognitive Developmental Approach to Socialization."

12. Rebecca Goodell, *Ethics in American Business: Policies, Programs and Perceptions* (Washington D.C.: Ethics Resource Center, 1994), 15.

13. Jeffrey A. Trachtenberg and Mark Robichaux, "Crooks Crack Digital Codes of Satellite TV," *The Wall Street Journal*, January 12, 1996, B1.

14. Neil C. Herndon, Debbie Thorne LeClair, and O.C. Ferrell, "Relationship of Individual Moral Values and Perceived Ethical Climate to Satisfaction, Commitment, and Turnover in a Sales Organization," working paper, The University of Tampa, Tampa, FL; and Randi

L. Sims and K. Galen Kroeck, "The Influence of Ethical Fit on Employee Satisfaction, Commitment and Turnover," *Journal of Business Ethics* 13 (December 1994): 939-947.

15. Margaret Kaeter, "Mission: Impossible?" *Business Ethics* 9 (January/February 1995): 24-26.

16. "SEC Charges Three in Kidder 1994 Bond Trading Scandal," *St. Petersburg Times*, January 10, 1996, 6E.

17. Mary Ellen Egan, "Old Enough to Know Better," *Business Ethics* 9 (January/February 1995): 19; and Greg Steinmetz, "Met Life Got Caught; Others Sent Same Letter," *The Wall Street Journal*, January 6, 1994, B1, B6.

Chapter 4

1. "Body, Mind and Spirit: The Sears Story," *Business Ethics* 10 (November/December 1996): 19-22.

2. Arts and Entertainment Network, "Investigative Reports," January 18, 1997.

3. William M. Frederick and James Weber, "The Value of Corporate Managers and Their Critics: An Empirical Description and Normative Implications," in *Research in Corporate Social Performance and Social Responsibility*, ed. William C. Frederick and Lee E. Preston (Greenwich, Conn.: JAI Press, 1987), 149-150.

4. Linda K. Trevino and Stuart Youngblood, "Bad Apples in Bad Barrels: Causal Analysis of Ethical Decision Making Behavior," *Journal of Applied Psychology* 75 (August 1990): 390.

5. Trevino and Youngblood, "Bad Apples in Bad Barrels," 400.

6. R. Eric Reidenbach and Donald P. Robin, *Ethics and Profits* (Englewood Cliffs, NJ: Prentice-Hall, 1989), 92.

7. Mark Maremont, "Abuse of Power: The Astonishing Tale of Sexual Harassment at Astra USA," *Business Week*, May 13, 1996, 86-98.

8. Reidenbach and Robin, *Ethics and Profits.*

9. Vikki Kratz, "Don't Be Shy," *Business*

Ethics 10 (January-February 1996): 15.

10. Mark Maremont, "Blind Ambition," *Business Week,* October 23, 1995, 78-92.

11. Lyman W. Porter, "Job Attitudes in Management: II. Perceived Importance of Needs as a Foundation of Job Level," *Journal of Applied Psychology* 47 (April 1963): 141-148.

12. Gene R. Laczniak and Patrick E. Murphy, *Ethical Marketing Decisions: The Higher Road* (Boston: Allyn & Bacon, 1993), 14.

13. Mark Pastin, "A Study of Organizational Factors and Their Effect on Compliance," in *Corporate Crime in America: Strengthening the "Good Citizen" Corporation* (Washington D.C.: United States Sentencing Commission), 175-179

Chapter 5

1. Laurie Hays, "Daiwa Bank Pleads Guilty to Conspiring to Hide Loss," *The Wall Street Journal,* February 29, 1996, A3; Jeffrey M. Kaplan, "Why Daiwa Bank Will Pay $340 Million Under the Sentencing Guidelines," *ethikos* 9 (May/ June 1996): 1–3, 11.

2. United States Sentencing Guidelines, § 8A.1. Washington, D.C.

3. Kaplan, "Why Daiwa Bank Will Pay $340 Million Under the Sentencing Guidelines," 2.

4. Richard P. Conaboy, "Corporate Crime in America: Strengthening the Good Citizen Corporation," in *Corporate Crime in America: Strengthening the "Good Citizen" Corporation* (Washington, D.C.: U.S. Sentencing Commission, 1995), 1–2.

5. Thomas Golden, "Employee Crime Can Cost You Millions," *Management Accounting,* August 1993, 39-44; Barbara Ettorre, "Crime and Punishment: A Hard Look at White-Collar Crime," *Management Review* 83 (May 1994): 10-16.

6. Alan R. Yuspeh, "Industry Practice: The Defense Industry Experience," *Compliance Programs and the Corporate Sentencing Guidelines – Preventing Criminal and Civil Liability,* Jeffrey M. Kaplan, Joseph E. Murphy, and Winthrop M. Swenson, eds. (Deerfield, IL: Clark Boardman Callaghan, 1994); and Alan R. Yuspeh, "Development of Corporate Compliance Programs: Lessons Learned from the DII Experience," in *Corporate Crime in America: Strengthening the "Good Citizen" Corporation* (Washington, D.C.: United States Sentencing Commission, 1995), 71–79.

7. Eleanor Hill, "Coordinating Enforcement Under the Department of Defense Voluntary Disclosure Program," in *Corporate Crime in America: Strengthening the "Good Citizen" Corporation* (Washington D.C.: United States Sentencing Commission, 1995), 287-294; and William B. Lytton, "The Case for Greater Coordination: Civil Sanctions and Third-Party Actions," in *Corporate Crime in America: Strengthening the "Good Citizen" Corporation* (Washington D.C.: United States Sentencing Commission, 1995), 295-304.

8. Win Swenson, "The Organizational Guidelines' `Carrot and Stick' Philosophy, and Their Focus on `Effective' Compliance," in *Corporate Crime in America: Strengthening the "Good Citizen" Corporation* (Washington D.C.: United States Sentencing Commission, 1995), 17–26.

9. Jay Sigler and Joseph Murphy, *Interactive Corporate Compliance: An Alternative to Regulatory Compulsion* (Greenwood Press, 1988).

10. Swenson, "The Organizational Guidelines' `Carrot and Stick' Philosophy," 17–26.

11. Bryan Gruley, "Little Town Becomes Municipality Sued by U.S. for Antitrust," *The Wall Street Journal,* June 3, 1996, A1.

12. United States Sentencing Guidelines, § 8A.1.

13. United States Sentencing Guidelines, § 8A.1.

14. USSG, § 8A.1.

15. Bryan Gruley, "ADM's $100 Million Price-Fixing Fine Blows Lid Off Usual Maximum Penalty," *The Wall Street Journal,* October 16, 1996, A4.

16. USSG, § 8A.1.

17. *Corporate Crime in America: Strengthening the "Good Citizen" Corporation* (Washington, D.C.: United States Sentencing Commission, 1995).

18. *Annual Reports* (Washington D.C.: United States Sentencing Commission, 1993, 1994, 1995).

19. John Scalia, Jr., "Cases Sentenced Under the Guidelines," in *Corporate Crime in America: Strengthening the "Good Citizen" Corporation* (Washington D.C.: United States Sentencing Commission, 1995), 253–268.

20. William S. Laufer, "A Study of Small Business Compliance Practices," in *Corporate Crime in America: Strengthening the "Good Citizen" Corporation* (Washington, D.C.: United States Sentencing Commission, 1995), 141–164.

21. Electric Supply of Tampa, Inc., May 1996.

22. United States Sentencing Commission, *Guidelines Manual,* § 3E1.1 (Washington, D.C.: United States Sentencing Commission, 1994).

23. USSG, § 8A.1.

24. NYNEX Office of Ethics and Business Conduct, "NYNEX Executive Commits Insider Trading Violation," *Ethics Leadership Review* 2 (Summer 1993): 2.

25. USSC, *Corporate Crime in America: Strengthening the "Good Citizen" Corporation.*

26. TECO Energy Inc., *Standards of Integrity* (Tampa, FL: TECO Energy Inc., 1993).

27. USSC, *Corporate Crime in America: Strengthening the 'Good Citizen' Corporation.*

28. Florida Progress Corporation *Code of Conduct* (St. Petersburg, FL: Office of Corporate Compliance, Florida Progress Corporation, 1995).

29. Clifford E. Dow and Robert G. Muehl, "Are Policies Keyed to New Sentencing Guidelines?" *Security Management* 36 (November 1992): 96-98.

30. Jeffrey M. Kaplan, "Liability Inventory," in *Compliance Programs and the Corporate Sentencing Guidelines–Preventing Criminal and Civil Liability,* Jeffrey M. Kaplan, Joseph E. Murphy, and Winthrop M. Swenson, eds. (Deerfield, IL: Clark Boardman Callaghan, 1994).

Chapter 6

1. Andrew W. Singer, "O&R's Ethics Council Includes All Levels of the Company," *ethikos* 10 (November/December 1996): 1-4, 15-16.

2. Denis Beauchamp, "The Canadian Defence Ethics Program and the 'Corporate Model'," *Federal Ethics Report* 4 (February 1997): 1.

3. John S. McClenahen, "Good Enough?" *Industry Week,* February 20, 1995, 58-62.

4. John R. Emshwiller, "Hot Special at Small Stores: Food Stamp Fraud," *The Wall Street Journal,* June 1, 1995, B1, B6.

5. Singer, "O&R's Ethics Council," 1.

6. Charlene Marmer Soloman, "Put Your Ethics to a Global Test," *Personnel Journal* 75 (January 1996): 66-74.

7. Curt S. Jordan, "Lessons in Organizational Compliance: A Survey of Government-Imposed Compliance Programs," *Preventive Law Reporter* 9 (Winter 1994): 4.

8. Michelle Neely Martinez, "HRM Update," *HR Magazine* 40 (December 1995): 16-17.

9. Andrew W. Singer, "Nortel's Code of Conduct: 'Hyperlink' on the World Wide Web," *ethikos* 9 (March/April 1996): 1.

10. Robert Howard, "Values Make the Company: An Interview with Robert Haas," *Harvard Business Review* 68

(September-October 1990): 134.

11. Susan Gaines, "Handing Out Halos," *Business Ethics* 8 (March-April 1994): 21.

12. Jordan, "Lessons in Organizational Compliance.

13. Read Hayes, "Retailers Toughen Ethics Codes to Curb Employee Abuses," *Stores,* July 1996, 83-84.

Chapter 7

1. Neil B. Hadley, "The Tenet Healthcare Corporation Experience in Developing an Ethics Education Program," presentation delivered at the Association for Practical and Professional Ethics conference, March 1997, Washington D.C.; and John Meyers, "Tenet Healthcare Corporation," in *Corporate Crime in America: Strengthening the "Good Citizen" Corporation* (Washington D.C.: United State Sentencing Commission, 1995), 69-80.

2. Mark Pastin, "A Study of Organizational Factors and Their Effect on Compliance," in *Corporate Crime in America: Strengthening the "Good Citizen" Corporation* (Washington, D.C.: United States Sentencing Commission, 1995), 175-185.

3. Barbara Ettorre, "Corporate Accountability 90s Style: The Buck Had Better Stop Here," *Management Review* 81 (April 1992): 16-21.

4. Ettorre, " Corporate Accountability 90s Style."

5. Edward Petry, "A Study of Compliance Practices in 'Compliance Aware' Companies," in *Corporate Crime in America: Strengthening the "Good Citizen" Corporation* (Washington, D.C.: United States Sentencing Commission, 1995), 139-158.

6. Linda K. Ferrell, "Gray Matters Ethics Training: An Evaluation," unpublished doctoral dissertation, 1996, University of Memphis.

7. KPMG Business Ethics Institute, "Keys to Effective Ethics Training," *Integrity*

(Fall 1996): 1, 3.

8. KPMG Business Ethics Institute, "Keys to Effective Ethics Training."

9. KPMG.

10. Charles C. Bonwell and James A. Eison, *Active Learning: Creating Excitement in the Classroom* (Washington, D.C.: Clearinghouse on Higher Education, 1991).

11. Timothy Mazur, "Training" in *Compliance Programs and the Corporate Sentencing Guidelines – Preventing Criminal and Civil Liability,* Jeffrey M. Kaplan, Joseph E. Murphy, and Winthrop M. Swenson, eds. (Deerfield, IL: Clark Boardman Callaghan, 1994).

12. "Intel's Lawyer in a Laptop Re-defining Corporate Compliance Training Programs," *Preventive Law Reporter* 9 (Winter 1994): 9.

13. "Interactive Video Takes Compliance Training to a New Level at GE," *ethikos* 5 (November/December 1992): 8.

14. Timothy T. Baldwin and J. Kevin Ford, "Transfer of Training: A Review and Directions for Future Research," *Personnel Psychology* 41 (1988): 63-105.

15. Tim C. Mazur, "Wendy's: Serving Up Ethics to Franchisees," *ethikos* 9 (March/April 1996): 6.

Chapter 8

1. "The GAP," *Business Ethics* 10 (May/June 1996): 1920.

2. David A. Ricks, *Big Business Blunders: Mistakes in International Marketing* (Homewood, Ill.: Dow-Jones Irwin, 1983), 83-84.

3. Ricks, *Big Business Blunders: Mistakes in International Marketing,* 16-18.

4. Joann S. Lublin, "Companies Use Cross-Cultural Training to Help Their Employees Adjust Abroad," *The Wall Street Journal,* August 4, 1993, B1, B6.

5. David P. Hamilton, "PC Makers Find China Is a Chaotic Market Despite Its Potential," *The Wall Street Journal,* March 4, 1996, A1, A9.

6. Dana Milbank and Marcus W. Brauchli, "Greasing Wheels," *The Wall Street Journal,* September 29, 1995, A1, A4.

7. Jennifer Cody, "To Forge Ahead, Career Women Are Venturing Out of Japan," *The Wall Street Journal,* August 29, 1994, B1, B5, C4.

8. William C. Frederick, "The Moral Authority of Transnational Corporate Codes," *Journal of Business Ethics* 10 (1991): 564-575.

9. Michael Williams, "Many Japanese Banks Ran Amok While Led by Former Regulators," *The Wall Street Journal,* January 19, 1996, A1, A9.

10. Bryan Gruley, "ADM's $100 Million Price-Fixing Fine Blows Lid Off Usual Maximum Penalty," *The Wall Street Journal,* October 16, 1996, A4; and Scott Kilman, Thomas M. Buton, and Richard Gibson, "An Executive Becomes Informant for the FBI, Stunning Giant ADM," *The Wall Street Journal,* July 10, 1995, A1.

11. Philip R. Cateora, *International Marketing* (Irwin, 1996), 568-569.

12. Rob Wells, "Bayer Unit Fined $50 Million for Criminal Price-Fixing," The Associated Press, January 30, 1997.

13. Jonathan Friedland, "Did IBM Unit Bribe Officials in Argentina to Land a Contract?" *The Wall Street Journal,* December 11, 1995, A1, A5.

14. Alix M. Freedman, "Cigarette Defector Says CEO Lied to Congress About View of Nicotine," *The Wall Street Journal,* January 26, 1996, A1, A4.

15. "Nestle Infant Formula: The Consequences of Spurning the Public Image," in *Marketing Mistakes,* 3rd ed., ed. Robert F. Hartley (Columbus, Ohio: Grid Publishing, 1986), 47-61; and "Nestle and the Role of Infant Formula in Developing Countries: The Resolution of a Conflict," a series of reports, articles, and press releases provided by Nestle Coordination Center for Nutrition, Inc., 1984.

16. Craig S. Smith, "China Becomes Industrial Nations' Most Favored Dump," *The Wall Street Journal,* October 9, 1995, B1.

17. "Phasers on 'Stun'," *Internet World* 8 (April 1997): 91.

18. Teri Agins, "Fashion Knockoffs Hit Stores Before Originals as Designers Seethe," *The Wall Street Journal,* August 8, 1994, A1, A3.

Chapter 9

1. Dale Kurschner, "5 Ways Ethical Busine$$ Creates Fatter Profit$," *Business Ethics* 10 (March/April 1996): 21.

2. Kurschner, "5 Ways Ethical Busine$$ Creates Fatter Profit$."

3. Archie B. Carroll, "The Pyramid of Corporate Social Responsibility: Toward the Moral Management of Organizational Stakeholders," *Business Horizons* 34 (July/August 1991): 42.

4. Dorothy J. Gaiter, "How Shoney's, Belted by a Lawsuit, Found the Path to Diversity," *The Wall Street Journal,* April 16, 1996, A1, A6.

5. Stephanie N. Mehta, "Black Entrepreneurs Benefit from Social Responsibility," *The Wall Street Journal,* October 19, 1995, B1, B2.

6. William M. Carley, "A Defense Contractor Gets Tough Scrutiny for Defective Products," *The Wall Street Journal,* February 27, 1996, A1.

7. "Putting Philosophy into Practice," Texas Instruments, Inc., pamphlet.

8. Lynn Sharp Paine, "Managing for Organizational Integrity," *Harvard Business Review* 72 (March-April 1994): 111.

9. Nelson Schwartz and Tim Smart, "Giving—and Getting Something Back," *Business Week,* August 28, 1995, 81.

10. Stan Crock, "When Charity Doesn't Begin at Home," *Business Week,* November 27, 1995, 34.

11. Schwartz and Smart, "Giving—and Getting Something Back."

12. Schwartz and Smart.

13. Dana Milbank, "Real Work: Hiring Welfare People, Hotel Chain Finds, Is Tough But Rewarding," *The Wall Street Journal*, October 31, 1996, A1, A10.

Chapter 10

1. Sources for the facts and excerpts used in discussing Hershey Foods include "Business Week's Industry Ranking for the S&P 500," *Business Week*, March 24, 1997, 130; "Hershey Foods Announces Fourth Quarter Results," *PR Newswire*, January 26, 1996; Hershey Foods Philosophy and Values," Hershey Foods Corporation videotape, 1990; Gary Hoover, Alta Campbell, and Patrick J. Spain, eds, *Hoover's Handbook* (Austin, TX: California Publishers Group West, 1991), 287; Karen Riley," Harmful Pleasures Put You at Risk of Paying More for Health Coverage," *Washington Times*, April 22, 1995, C1; Steven S. Ross, "Green Groceries," *Mother Jones* 14 (February-March 1989): 48-49; and "A Tradition of Excellence," Hershey Foods Corporation, August 1990.

2. Sources for the facts and excerpts used in discussing Lockheed Martin include "Business Week's Industry Ranking for the S&P 500," *Business Week*, March 24, 1997, 120; and Lockheed Martin Office of Ethics and Business Conduct, *Ethics Matters*, December 1996.

3. Sources for the facts and excerpts used in discussing Waste Management include "Business Week's Industry Ranking for the S&P 500," *Business Week*, March 24, 1997, 146; Subrata Chakravarty, "Dean Buntrock's Green Machine," *Forbes*, August 2, 1993, 96-100; Christel Cothran, "Proactive Environmental Activity Eases Permitting Process," *Journal of Environmental Permitting* (Summer 1993): 293-300; "Ethics in Our Workplace: Guidelines for Our People," Waste Management Technologies code of ethics booklet, 1993; Gary Hoover, Alta Campbell, and Patrick Spain, eds., *Hoover's Handbook of American Businesses* (Austin, Tex.: The Reference Press, 1994), 1130-1131; Kevin Kearney,

"Process Safety Management," *Professional Safety*, August 1993, 16-22; and Lynn Sharp Paine, "Managing for Organizational Integrity," *Harvard Business Review* 72 (March-April 1994): 106-111.

4. Sources for the facts and excerpts used in discussing Texas Instruments include "Business Week's Industry Ranking for the S&P 500," *Business Week*, March 24, 1997, 128; "Cornerstone," Ethics Office, Texas Instruments Inc., 1988; "Ethics in the Business of TI," Texas Instruments Incorporated, 1987; Texas Instruments Inc., 1995 Annual Report, Dallas TX; "Building on the Cornerstone of Ethics," Texas Instruments Inc., pamphlet, 1996; "The Networked Society," Texas Instruments Inc., pamphlet, 1996; "Working Globally," Texas Instruments Inc., pamphlet; "Ethical and Leadership 2000," Texas Instruments Inc., pamphlet, 1996.

5. Sources for the facts and excerpts used in discussing Home Depot include "Business Week's Industry Ranking for the S&P 500," *Business Week*, March 24, 1997, 124; *Painting the Industry Orange*, The Home Depot 1995 Annual Report, Atlanta, GA; Edward A. Robinson, "America's Most Admired Companies," *Fortune*, March 3, 1997, 68-75; and *Social Responsibility Report 1995*, The Home Depot, Atlanta, GA.

6. Anne Gill, "Telecommunications Industry Practice Forum," in *Corporate Crime in America: Strengthening the "Good Citizen" Corporation* (Washington, D.C.: United States Sentencing Commission, 1995), 89-92.

7. "Glass Ceiling at Home Depot?" *Business Week*, April 7, 1997, 47.

8. Dale Kurschner, "5 Ways Ethical Busine$$ Creates Fatter Profit$," *Business Ethics* 10 (March/April 1996): 20-23.

9. Kurschner, "5 Ways Ethical Busine$$ Creates Fatter Profit$,"; and "Does It Pay to Be Ethical?" *Business Ethics* 11 (March/April 1997): 14-16.

INDEX

ON THE WEB

Visit our Web site at:

http://www.utampa.edu/acad/cob/cfe/orginteg.htm

This Web site provides a continuous flow of new ideas to help you improve your organization's integrity efforts. We recommend that you use the Web site to find additional information on chapters that are of particular importance. This Web site makes the book interactive, so please feel free to E-Mail us and communicate about effective integrity initiatives in your organization.